EASY
INDIAN
VEGETARIAN

EASY INDIAN VEGETARIAN

**Delicious recipes
for every day**

CHETNA MAKAN

hamlyn

TO SIA AND YUV. WATCHING YOU GROW INTO SUCH BEAUTIFUL PEOPLE KEEPS ME GOING!

First published in Great Britain in 2024 by Hamlyn,
an imprint of Octopus Publishing Group Ltd
Carmelite House
50 Victoria Embankment
London EC4Y 0DZ
www.octopusbooks.co.uk

An Hachette UK Company
www.hachette.co.uk

Text copyright © Chetna Makan 2024
Design & layout copyright © Octopus Publishing Group Ltd 2024

Distributed in the US by
Hachette Book Group
1290 Avenue of the Americas
4th and 5th Floors
New York, NY 10104

Distributed in Canada by
Canadian Manda Group
664 Annette St.
Toronto, Ontario, Canada M6S 2C8

ISBN 978-0-600-63775-2

A CIP catalogue record for this book is available from the British Library.

Printed and bound in China.

10 9 8 7 6 5 4 3 2 1

Editorial Director: Natalie Bradley
Art Director: Juliette Norsworthy
Senior Editor: Leanne Bryan
Copy Editor: Emily Preece-Morrison
Photographer: Nassima Rothacker
Food Stylist: Rosie Reynolds
Props Stylist: Lauren Miller
Production Manager: Caroline Alberti

CONTENTS

Introduction 6

Snacks 15

Veg 51

Dal 89

Flatbreads 113

Rice 141

Sides 161

Sweet 185

Menu plans 208

Glossary of UK/US terms 216

Index 218

Acknowledgements 223

About the author 224

Introduction

Food, especially Indian food, has meant something more than just 'food' to me in the last few years. Moving to the UK 20 years ago, to a sleepy town on the Kent coast, I found I missed the food – the hustle and bustle of street vendors, the warmth of Indian kitchens and all the delicious meals that accompanied them. It made me want to learn more about Indian cookery, to take notes from my family and friends whenever I visited them, and to look at and taste everything with more intensity. What followed were my last seven cookbooks, talking about everyday healthy Indian food, Indian street food, quick Indian food, and more.

Throughout this journey, I have tried not to focus on any one particular cuisine of India. We all know that there are many types of Indian food – it's like the variety of all the cuisines of Europe, but condensed into one country – that's how varied and vast it is. So instead of focussing on a particular regional cuisine, I drew inspiration from different parts of India and my own life experiences to recreate a diverse collection of recipes and in the process create new ones too.

I have now reached a point where I want to explore flavours and tastes that are new to me. Being a Punjabi, born and brought up in Madhya Pradesh, and then studying and working among the very mixed communities in Mumbai, I have been lucky to experience a wide variety of Indian food already, for which I am very grateful. But for this book I wanted to venture to somewhere I haven't travelled before, not just in terms of place but also food. I wanted to learn more about everyday vegetarian cooking – the reasons behind it, the flavours, the techniques, and also about the people creating it all day, every day, for their families.

It's very natural to Indian culture to just cook vegetarian meals. It's not about trying to replace meat or fish with veg, but rather the simple act of creating healthy and delicious meals that just happen to be vegetarian – that is what I find beautiful and inspiring. So much flavour is found in Indian spices and herbs, local vegetables and lentils, that never a thought is given to meat or any substitutes. People have all the right potions to create vegetarian magic day in, day out.

My journey led me to Ahmedabad in Gujarat, a state famous for its lively vegetarian food. In the process of looking for home cooks who would be happy to share their knowledge with me, I met Sheetal Bhatt. Sheetal is not just a passionate cook, but is doing something truly commendable: exploring the native foods of Gujarat, documenting the fast-vanishing food practices and traditions of Gujarati cuisine, and promoting healthy, home-cooked meals. Meeting her was my lucky break that opened the doors to many kitchens in Ahmedabad, from Sheetal's friends to her cousins. Everyone welcomed me with so much love and warmth, and I will be forever grateful to them for the experience of watching them create magic in their kitchens. This is my chance to share a little bit about them with you.

My first visit was to Avani's home, an attractive, warm family home with an equally welcoming kitchen, packed with jars of ingredients, old and beautiful kitchen equipment, and much more – her passion for cooking! Avani Mehta is a talented and experienced cook who follows Jainism and is very proud of its principles and values. She cooks fresh meals for her family every single day, and everything is homemade, from breakfast and lunch to dinner and all the snacks in between. Within a few minutes of arriving, she had cooked the most delicious lunch for me, complete with dal, flatbreads and even sweets. It was a joy to watch her move around her kitchen with such free-flowing charm and elegance.

Avani shared a lot about Jainism with me while she was cooking. Jainism teaches non-violence and reducing harm to all living things, so a vegetarian diet that inflicts the least amount of harm is followed. Jains have a strict list of dos and don'ts when it comes to what they should and should not eat. They don't eat anything that is grown under the soil – one of the reasons being that, when you pull the plant to eat the vegetable, you are destroying the habitat and causing harm to any living beings that live around and in that soil. Jains also believe that as the sun does not touch a subterranean vegetable, that makes it unhealthy. They don't eat any sprouted food, which they believe causes harm to the body, and prefer to skip vegetables for 11 days in a month, the idea being that it gives the body a break from those vegetables and lets it balance out within. They believe that consuming milk in the evenings is beneficial for your body and they don't combine yogurt with other foods, preferring to eat it on its own to get the most out of it.

Jains eat 48 minutes after sunrise – a practice called *navkarshi* – and the time of sunrise is published every day in the newspaper so that people can follow it easily. They also follow *chowvihar*, which means they stop eating after sunset (also known as *ratri bhojan tyaag*, which means giving up the evening meal). This is something that really got me thinking about intermittent fasting. It may be a new fashion in Western food, but don't the roots of it lie in Jainist principles? Like a lot of things, it has been taken up from Indian culture and served to the world under new packaging. Rather than being an amazing Western discovery, intermittent fasting has in fact been practised by Jains for centuries!

An important saying in the Jain culture is *jeeva matte khau, khava matte na jeevo*, which translates to 'eat to live and not live to eat' (although, personally, I follow just the opposite practice!). Seasonal eating is key. After springtime, Jains stop eating the leafy green vegetables that are on their way out after winter.

They believe that the body cannot digest these after a certain season, and that they should move on to the summer vegetables after that. Sticking with seasonal produce is something that I would love to practise too. These ancient principles make perfect sense in today's world.

My second stop was Meena Aunty's home, which had that old-world charm with some of the furniture style I remember from my grandparents' house. It made me feel very nostalgic. Her kitchen was dreamy and what I loved the most were the very organised drawers of pans, spoons, plates and bowls. Wow, what a collection and what an organised kitchen! Having cooked all her life, Meena Aunty could probably do so with her eyes closed. She told me how, when she was married, she came to live in a joint family with her brothers, sisters-in-law and their kids and they would all cook in turns and together as a team. Now, it's just her and her daughter in the same house and it is full of memories. She cooked an amazing thali for me, with so many little treats that I didn't know what to eat first. Everything tasted so balanced and perfect.

My next stop was Bhumika's home, which she shares with her husband. She had moved to the house recently and had made a little garden, growing a few vegetables, herbs and fruit. Bhumika Udernani is a writer and loves to cook. From a Sindhi background, she is trying to learn more about and perfect Sindhi vegetarian food. She shared some lovely stories about her family and their food while she made a stunning Sindhi feast for me.

The following day, I went to meet Kety Aunty, an extraordinary woman in her 70s who runs the Zoroastrian Ladies Industrial Cooperative Society, which provides Parsi meals, snacks and masalas to the community. She had such a big smile on her face the whole afternoon and tons of energy interacting with her kitchen team, which comprised a group of Gujarati women (not Parsi), something that surprised me. After chatting to them, I found out that some of these women had been working in that kitchen for over 25 years. When they joined, they used to help the Parsi women cook and, through that process, learned all the recipes and techniques. Slowly, the Parsi women got older and retired, and now the kitchen is run by the Gujarati crew, and that in itself is a marvel. They had such a good rapport with each other, laughing and sharing jokes while cooking. They cooked a few delicious Parsi treats, things that I had never had before and that you cannot find on the internet today, and I will never forget my afternoon in that kitchen with that lovely bunch.

My next stop was Sheetal's family home, where I was welcomed by Renuka Vikas Chauhan and her lovely family. We went straight to the kitchen where she started cooking dinner for me while chatting and telling me about the food. In no time, the dinner was on the table without her breaking a sweat. She told me that she has been making most of the dishes she cooked for years. They were dishes that her family could not do without, and some were needed every day in their meals. I was stunned by the speed of her cooking and the beautiful thali that she created. It was so lovely to hear stories from her mother-in-law, Nanda Ba, who accompanied us into the kitchen, where she sat on a chair and oversaw everything. They once lived in a big extended family. Slowly, the children married, the older generation passed away, and now just a single family was left there. What caught my attention was a cupboard full of utensils

that had belonged to all the different family members. Kitchen utensils that the ladies brought with them when they got married, each one speaking a different story about a different generation.

The next day we met Shimul, a talented and inspiring lady who not only runs her own travel business but is a very passionate cook. A few years ago, she started making pickles at home, just once a year in the summer season. Shimul's mother had been a great cook. Shimul realised that she was losing her mum's recipes and people were missing out on the amazing things she cooked. To keep her mum's memory alive, she started making her pickles, which are now very popular the world over. She only takes limited orders because she wants to make them all herself at home. Once they are sold, you have to wait until next year for more. I tried the pickles while visiting and was blown away, both by them and by her effortless cooking and the most delicious spread she served. Her stunning home is one of the few old buildings still standing in the midst of all the new developments in Ahmedabad and I hope it stays that way, with all its old-world charm and beauty.

My last stop of the trip was to visit Ranjan Aunty, who lives with her children. She still cooks for them all and insists on making fresh food for all mealtimes. She was so quick and fluent in the kitchen and it filled me with so much joy to watch her cook. Once she had cooked the food, she cleared the work surface and perched herself comfortably on top to roll out the theplas like a machine conveyor belt – such skill.

This book is not just about Gujarati or Sindhi or Parsi food – it has influences from all over India, including some Punjabi and South Indian food, too. I stopped in Mumbai on my way back from Gujarat to visit my college friend Lakshmi, who invited me to her mum's kitchen so that I could learn a thing or two about South Indian cuisine. It was such joy to catch up with my friend after more than a decade, but to be able do it while watching her mum, Subbalakshmi Gopalkrishnan, cook was like a dream. She made us an absolute feast. Some of the things I sadly could not include in the book, as the ingredients are not available outside India, but I have tried to capture her flavours instead.

In Mumbai I also stopped at my cousin Nimisha's house. Growing up, we spent a lot of time together in the summer holidays and I love visiting her. She is married to Prashant from Hyderabad and cooks a lot of recipes passed down by her mother-in-law. As always, she was happy to cook for me this time too. Being Punjabi, it is such a joy to watch her cook Hyderabadi dishes with such ease now.

My final stop was at my friend's house, close to my home. Radhika Mangam is a GP by profession and loves to cook for her family and friends. I am very lucky to have had many meals prepared by her. Every time she cooks something that I haven't tried before, I am right there with my pen and paper taking notes.

Writing this book has been an adventure, with long, tiring days spent getting those flavours as close as possible to the real thing I ate in India, but it has given me endless joy to put it together. Whether you try one or ten recipes from the book, I hope it will bring happiness to you and your families, and I hope I have done justice to all the recipes that were kindly handed to me with so much love and pride.

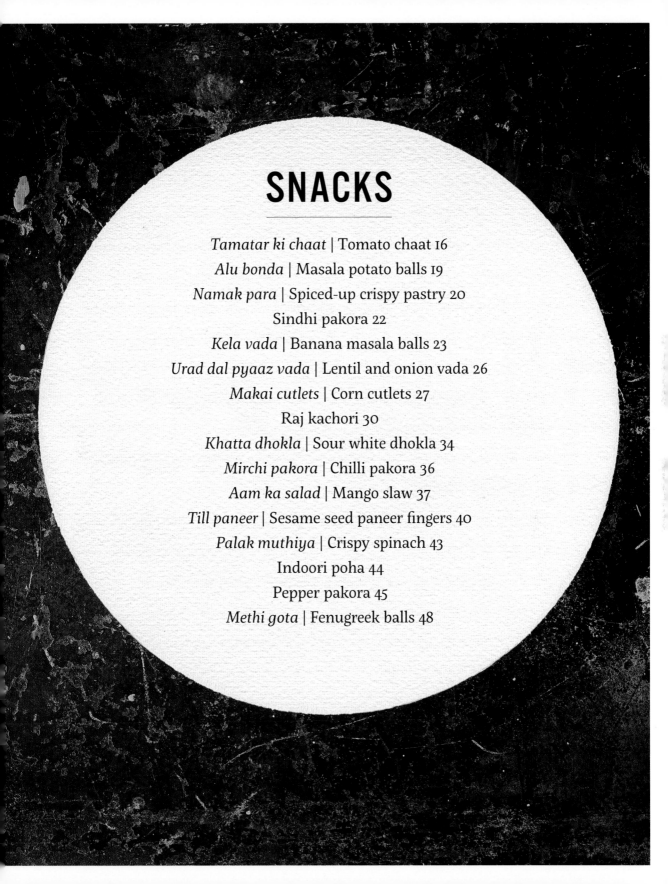

SNACKS

Tamatar ki chaat | Tomato chaat 16

Alu bonda | Masala potato balls 19

Namak para | Spiced-up crispy pastry 20

Sindhi pakora 22

Kela vada | Banana masala balls 23

Urad dal pyaaz vada | Lentil and onion vada 26

Makai cutlets | Corn cutlets 27

Raj kachori 30

Khatta dhokla | Sour white dhokla 34

Mirchi pakora | Chilli pakora 36

Aam ka salad | Mango slaw 37

Till paneer | Sesame seed paneer fingers 40

Palak muthiya | Crispy spinach 43

Indoori poha 44

Pepper pakora 45

Methi gota | Fenugreek balls 48

There are many types of *chaat* in India, some documented and many thousands not. Tomato chaat is something that started in Banaras and since then has taken some different forms. Here is my take on the famous Banarasi tomato chaat and I hope I do justice to it. It's light, refreshing and perfect as a snack or summer meal.

Tamatar ki chaat | Tomato chaat

Heat the oil in a large pan and add the cumin seeds. Once they start to sizzle, add the ginger and cook for a minute, then add the chilli and cashew nuts and cook for 2 minutes. Add all the spices, then after a few seconds add the tomatoes. Cook over a medium heat for 5 minutes until they start to soften.

Add the boiling water to the pan, then add the sugar and salt, cover and cook for 10 minutes. Add the crushed potatoes and bring to the boil. Once the potatoes are heated through, add the fresh coriander.

Transfer the mixture to serving bowls, drizzle with some chutney and sprinkle a little Bombay mix on top, then serve.

SERVES 4

4 tablespoons sunflower oil

1 teaspoon cumin seeds

2.5cm (1 inch) piece of fresh root ginger, peeled and finely chopped

1 green chilli, finely chopped

50g (1¾oz) cashew nuts, roughly chopped

1 teaspoon chilli powder

1 teaspoon ground turmeric

1 teaspoon ground cumin

1 teaspoon ground coriander

1 teaspoon garam masala

1 teaspoon mango powder (amchur)

½ teaspoon black salt (kala namak)

8 tomatoes, roughly chopped

200ml (7fl oz) boiling water

½ teaspoon caster sugar

½ teaspoon salt

2 medium potatoes, boiled and gently crushed

a handful of fresh coriander, finely chopped

TO SERVE

Coriander and Ginger Chutney (see page 172)

Bombay mix

A great snack, these *alu bondas* are a delight. *Alu bonda* is another name for *alu vada*. *Vada* is what these potato fritters are called in Mumbai and *bonda* is what they are called in Madhya Pradesh, where I grew up. Whatever you choose to call them, I would recommend you try to make these and enjoy them with some Coriander and Ginger Chutney or Onion and Garlic Chutney.

Alu bonda | Masala potato balls

MAKES 16

sunflower oil, for deep-frying

sea salt flakes, to garnish

Coriander and Ginger Chutney (see page 172) or Onion and Garlic Chutney (see page 176), to serve

FOR THE POTATO FILLING

4 medium potatoes, boiled and mashed

½ teaspoon salt

½ teaspoon chilli powder

½ teaspoon chaat masala

½ teaspoon ground cumin

10g (¼oz) fresh dill, chopped

10g (¼oz) fresh coriander, chopped

1 red onion, finely chopped

FOR THE BATTER

150g (5½oz) gram flour (besan), sieved

½ teaspoon salt

½ teaspoon ground turmeric

½ teaspoon chilli powder

175ml (6fl oz) water

To prepare the potato filling, put the mashed potatoes into a bowl, add the rest of the filling ingredients and mix well. Divide into 16 equal portions, then form the portions into balls and flatten them.

Put all the ingredients for the batter in a separate bowl and mix until smooth.

Heat enough oil for deep-frying in a large, deep pan to 170°C (340°F) or until a cube of bread browns in 25 seconds when dropped into the oil. When the oil is hot enough, dip the potato *bonda* into the batter and carefully lower into the hot oil (you will need to do this in batches so the temperature of the oil doesn't reduce too much). Cook for 3–4 minutes, turning halfway through, until golden and crispy. Remove with a slotted spoon to drain on kitchen paper.

Sprinkle with sea salt flakes and serve hot with your choice of chutney.

These snacks can be found all over India – they all taste different and that's the beauty of them. I grew up with the very Punjabi *namak paras* and when I went to Gujarat and tried these amazing Gujarati *namak paras*, I was blown away. So balanced with the perfect level of spice, these *namak paras* are inspired by the ones I had at Avani's house. She also gave me a little box of them to take back home with me; how I love Indian hospitality!

Namak para | Spiced-up crispy pastry

SERVES 8

200g (7oz) chapatti flour

50g (1¾oz) plain flour

½ teaspoon salt

½ teaspoon chilli powder

½ teaspoon soft brown sugar

2 tablespoons dried fenugreek leaves (kasuri methi)

2 teaspoons sesame seeds

1 teaspoon onion seeds

¼ teaspoon bicarbonate of soda

4 tablespoons peanut oil, plus extra to drizzle

about 125ml (4fl oz) water

sunflower oil, for deep-frying

Chilli Chutney (see page 173), to serve

Put all the dry ingredients in a large bowl and mix together. Now add the peanut oil and rub it in well until you have a breadcrumb texture. Slowly add the water until you have a soft dough – you might need a little less or more. Knead for a few seconds, then drizzle over a few more drops of peanut oil and rub it on top. Cover the dough and leave to rest for 30 minutes.

Divide the dough into 8 equal portions and roll out each portion to a thin disc about 2mm (¹⁄₁₆ inch) thick. Prick all over with a fork so they don't puff up while frying, then cut each disc into diamond shapes, as big as you like.

Heat enough oil for deep-frying in a large, deep pan to around 160°C (320°F), or until a cube of bread browns in 45 seconds when dropped into the oil. Fry the *namak para* in batches for 3–4 minutes, turning halfway through, until golden and crispy. Remove with a slotted spoon to drain on kitchen paper and let cool before serving with some Chilli Chutney.

You can store these in an airtight container for up to 2 weeks.

It was only when I was chatting to Bhumika about Sindhi food that I found out about these delicious Sindhi pakoras. Until then, I had no idea that they made pakoras in a different way. The batter is first fried in big clumps and then broken into smaller pieces and fried again until crisp. They are super crunchy and delicious. You can make the larger clumps beforehand, then break them down to fry again just before serving with some Tomato Chutney or Coriander and Ginger Chutney.

Sindhi pakora

SERVES 4

1 teaspoon cumin seeds

2 tablespoons coriander seeds

5 onions, roughly chopped

1 teaspoon salt

½ teaspoon ground turmeric

200g (7oz) gram flour (besan)

125ml (4fl oz) water

sunflower oil, for deep-frying

Tomato Chutney (see page 166) or Coriander and Ginger Chutney (see page 172), to serve

Dry roast the cumin and coriander seeds in a hot frying pan for 2 minutes until they change colour and get nicely roasted. Transfer to a pestle and mortar and crush them roughly.

Add the crushed seeds to a large bowl with the remaining ingredients, except for the water and sunflower oil. Slowly add the water. The batter for these pakoras is not runny but very sticky.

Heat the oil for deep-frying in a large, deep pan to around 160°C (320°F), or until a cube of bread browns in 45 seconds when dropped into the oil. Once it is hot enough, put clumps of the batter, roughly 5–7.5cm (2–3 inches) in diameter into the hot oil. Cook for 2 minutes until beginning to get some colour, then remove with a slotted spoon to drain on kitchen paper. Repeat until all the batter has been fried.

Now increase the heat of the oil to 170°C (340°F). Break the large clumps of pakora into 4 pieces each and fry again for 2 minutes until crispy and golden. Remove to drain on kitchen paper once again.

Serve hot with your choice of chutney.

These *vadas* are a popular snack and a great alternative to *alu* (potato) *vadas* for people who don't eat potatoes. When I met Avani, whose family follows the Jain religion, she told me about the many foods that they don't eat, potatoes being one of them. Make sure to buy your green bananas from an Asian shop and not regular slightly hard green bananas from a supermarket. Serve with Coriander and Ginger Chutney.

Kela vada | Banana masala balls

MAKES 16

sunflower oil, for deep-frying

sea salt flakes, to garnish

Coriander and Ginger Chutney (see page 172), to serve

FOR THE BANANAS

7 raw green bananas

2 tablespoons peanut oil

1 teaspoon salt

½ teaspoon sugar

2 green chillies, finely chopped

1 tablespoon lemon juice

FOR THE TEMPERING

2 tablespoons peanut oil

1 teaspoon mustard seeds

2 teaspoons urad dal (white lentils)

10 curry leaves, chopped

¼ teaspoon asafoetida

½ teaspoon ground turmeric

FOR THE BATTER

125g (4½oz) gram flour (besan)

½ teaspoon salt

½ teaspoon ground turmeric

a pinch of asafoetida

160ml (5½fl oz) water

Put the whole unpeeled bananas in a pan and cover with water. Add the peanut oil to the pan and bring to the boil, then reduce to a simmer for 45 minutes. Leave to cool slightly, then peel the bananas and grate them into a bowl. Add the salt, sugar, chillies and lemon juice.

Heat the oil for the tempering in a large pan, add the mustard seeds and urad dal and cook over a low heat for 1 minute. Stir in the curry leaves, asafoetida and turmeric, then add the banana mixture and cook for a further 5 minutes. Leave to cool slightly.

Divide the cooled banana mixture into 16 pieces and shape these into balls.

Put all the ingredients for the batter in a bowl and whisk until smooth. This should not be a watery batter – it should be thick enough to coat the *vada*.

Heat enough oil for deep-frying in a large, deep pan to 170°C (340°F) or until a cube of bread browns in 25 seconds when dropped into the oil. When the oil is hot enough, dip each banana *vada* into the batter, coat well and carefully lower into the hot oil (you will need to do this in batches so the temperature of the oil doesn't reduce too much). Cook for 4–5 minutes until golden, then remove with a slotted spoon to drain on kitchen paper.

Sprinkle with sea salt flakes and serve hot with the Coriander and Ginger Chutney.

These should come with a warning that you can't eat just one. I have tried these *vadas* at my friend Radhika's house, who is originally from Hyderabad and lives locally to me. Everytime she makes them, I can't stop eating them, so it's only fair that I share her recipe with you. Enjoy these with Onion and Garlic Chutney.

Urad dal pyaaz vada | Lentil and onion vada

MAKES 20

300g (10½oz) urad dal (white lentils)

1 onion, thinly sliced

100g (3½oz) cabbage, grated

½ teaspoon salt

½ teaspoon chilli powder

a handful of fresh coriander, finely chopped

1 green chilli, finely chopped

10 curry leaves, chopped

sunflower oil, for deep-frying and greasing

Onion and Garlic Chutney (see page 176), to serve

Soak the dal in water overnight.

The next day, drain the dal and blitz it to a paste in a food processor. You might need a tablespoon or so of water to help loosen it, but don't add too much as you want a thick paste.

Transfer the paste to a bowl and mix in all the other ingredients, apart from the oil. Mix well.

Heat enough oil for deep-frying in a large, deep pan to around 150–160°C (300–320°F), or until a cube of bread browns in 45 seconds when dropped into the oil. (Too hot oil would cook the *vada* on the outside but not in the middle.)

Pour a little oil into the palm of your hand, then take a scoop of the mixture in your hand and slightly flatten it.

Dip your finger in some water and poke a hole all the way through the centre of the *vada*. Carefully peel it away from your hand and lower it into the hot oil. Cook for 5–6 minutes, turning halfway through, until crispy and golden. Remove with a slotted spoon to drain on kitchen paper.

Repeat to cook all the *vadas* in this way, cooking them in batches so the oil temperature does not get too low.

If you find this technique a bit tricky, just use a spoon to scoop the mixture straight into the oil.

Serve these hot with my Onion and Garlic Chutney.

Quick snacks don't need to be boring when you have things like these corn cutlets, which are so delicious. I use frozen sweetcorn here, but if you can find fresh seasonal sweetcorn then feel free to use that instead. Adjust the heat to your taste and serve them hot with an equally fabulous chutney.

Makai cutlets | Corn cutlets

MAKES 12

sunflower oil, for deep-frying

sea salt flakes, to garnish

your choice of chutney, to serve

FOR THE CUTLETS

1 teaspoon coriander seeds

1 teaspoon cumin seeds

1 teaspoon fennel seeds

1 teaspoon chilli flakes

400g (14oz) frozen sweetcorn

1 onion, finely chopped

1 green chilli, finely chopped

½ teaspoon garam masala

¾ teaspoon salt

50g (1¾oz) breadcrumbs

a handful of fresh coriander, finely chopped

3 tablespoons cornflour

Put the coriander, cumin and fennel seeds in a pestle and mortar along with the chilli flakes and crush coarsely.

Put the frozen sweetcorn in a saucepan and cover with boiling water. Let it sit for 5 minutes, then drain. Transfer the sweetcorn to a food processor and blitz to a coarse paste, but don't purée it. Transfer the paste to a bowl, add the spices and remaining cutlet ingredients and mix well.

Heat enough oil for deep-frying in a large, deep pan to 170°C (340°F) or until a cube of bread browns in 25 seconds when dropped into the oil. When the oil is hot enough, take small portions of the mixture, slightly flatten and fry for 2–3 minutes, turning halfway through, until golden and crispy. Remove with a slotted spoon to drain on kitchen paper and repeat with the remaining mixture.

Sprinkle the cutlets with sea salt flakes and serve them hot with your choice of chutney.

Raj means 'royal' and this raj kachori very much deserves that title. Thought to have originated in Rajasthan, the dish seems to have been made for the royal family and slowly spread to the rest of India in the form of a very popular street food. The crispy *kachori* is the perfect vessel for so many textures and flavours; this is a meal you will not forget quickly. You can prepare all the elements beforehand and bring them together just before serving.

Raj kachori

MAKES 8

FOR THE DAL

200g (7oz) whole moong dal (mung beans)

800ml (1 pint 9fl oz) water

½ teaspoon salt

½ teaspoon chilli powder

FOR THE *KACHORI* DOUGH

150g (5½oz) fine semolina

150g (5½oz) plain flour, plus extra for dusting

½ teaspoon salt

½ teaspoon ground turmeric

¼ teaspoon bicabonate of soda

1 tablespoon sunflower oil, plus extra for deep-frying

150ml (5fl oz) water

FOR THE YOGURT

400g (14oz) natural yogurt

150ml (5fl oz) water

½ teaspoon salt

½ teaspoon icing sugar

Start by soaking the moong dal in a saucepan with the water for 1 hour, then bring to the boil and cook for 30–40 minutes until soft and broken up and all the water has been absorbed. Add the salt and chilli powder, and mix well. Set aside to cool.

Meanwhile, prepare the *kachori* dough. Put all the dry ingredients in a bowl and mix well. Add the oil, then slowly add the water, just enough to make a soft dough. You might need a bit more or less water. Knead for 1 minute, then cover and leave to rest for 30 minutes.

Meanwhile, mix together the yogurt ingredients, and prepare or gather the rest of the serving ingredients.

Divide the dough into 8 equal portions. Roll out each portion on a flour-dusted work surface to a rough disc, 15cm (6 inches) in diameter.

Heat enough oil for deep-frying in a large, deep saucepan to 170°C (340°F) or until a cube of bread browns in 25 seconds when dropped into the oil. When the oil is hot enough, gently put a *kachori* into the oil and let it puff up. Now reduce the heat and

TO SERVE

4 potatoes, boiled and cut into tiny pieces

400g (14oz) tin of chickpeas, drained and rinsed

chilli powder

Tamarind Chutney (see page 179)

Coriander and Ginger Chutney (see page 172)

a handful of fresh coriander leaves

fine sev

Bombay mix

a handful of pomegranate seeds

1 small beetroot, julienned

salt

cook for 2 minutes on each side until crispy and golden. Remove with a slotted spoon to cool and drain on kitchen paper.

Repeat until all the *kachori* are cooked, bringing the oil back up to temperature each time you start a new one, then reducing the temperature as it cooks.

Assemble when you are ready to serve. Place a *kachori* on a plate and break open the top of it. Put some dal in it, followed by some potatoes. Drizzle over lots of yogurt, followed by some chickpeas, then sprinkle with a pinch of salt and chilli powder. Drizzle over more yogurt, then follow with a drizzle of the chutneys, fresh coriander, sev, Bombay mix, pomegranate seeds and julienned beetroot. Serve.

Khatta means 'sour' and this *dhokla* gets its name as the batter used to make it is left to ferment overnight with yogurt. There are many kinds of *dhoklas* – I have chosen the one I like the most: it is dense and has an earthiness to it with the gentle flavours of chilli and ginger. The recipe for the flour mix came from Sheetal and the technique was shown to me by Shimul – both amazing cooks.

Khatta dhokla | Sour white dhokla

SERVES 4–6

200g (7oz) basmati rice

60g (2¼oz) chana dal (split yellow peas)

30g (1oz) toor dal (split pigeon peas)

200g (7oz) natural yogurt

200ml (7fl oz) water

1cm (½ inch) piece of fresh root ginger, peeled and finely chopped

½ teaspoon salt

¼ teaspoon bicarbonate of soda

1 green chilli, finely chopped

sunflower oil, for greasing

a pinch of chilli powder

a pinch of ground cumin

Coriander and Ginger Chutney (see page 172), to serve (optional)

Dry roast the rice and dals in a dry pan over a low heat for 5 minutes until they become aromatic and start to change colour. Set aside to cool.

Blitz the cooled rice and dals to a coarse powder the texture of semolina in a food processor. Add the yogurt and water to the powder, stir well, cover and leave to rest overnight.

The next day, add the ginger, salt, bicarbonate of soda and fresh chilli to the fermented mixture and mix well.

Grease 2 round cake tins, 15cm (6 inches) across, or 1 large 30cm (12 inch) cake tin. Fill the tin(s) with the batter and sprinkle the chilli powder and cumin on top.

Place the cake tin(s) in a steamer pan (or a large pan with a lid, with an upturned heatproof bowl or metal trivet placed inside). Fill the pan with a shallow depth of boiling water, then place over the heat and steam for 15 minutes. Check whether the *dhokla* is done by inserting a knife – if it comes out clean, then it's cooked.

Leave to cool in the tin for 2 minutes, then cut into diamond shapes and remove from the tin. Serve with some Coriander and Ginger Chutney, if liked.

These pakora might sound hot and dangerous but they are deliciously mild. I use green Thai chillies, which have just a gentle heat, stuffed with spiced potatoes and coated in batter to give them a soft filling with a crispy coating on the outside. Serve with some Tamarind Chutney for a sour and sweet accompaniment; Coriander and Ginger Chutney is lovely too.

Mirchi pakora | Chilli pakora

MAKES 20

2 medium potatoes, boiled and mashed

¼ teaspoon salt

¼ teaspoon chilli powder

¼ teaspoon garam masala

¼ teaspoon ground coriander

¼ teaspoon ground cumin

20 green Thai or Serrano chillies

sunflower oil, for deep-frying

Tamarind Chutney (see page 179) or Coriander and Ginger Chutney (see page 172), to serve

FOR THE BATTER

125g (4½oz) gram flour (besan)

¼ teaspoon salt

¼ teaspoon ground turmeric

a pinch of asafoetida

140–150ml (4½–5fl oz) water

Combine the mashed potatoes, salt and all the spices in a bowl and mix well.

Make a slit in the middle of each chilli (no need to deseed) and stuff the cavity of each one with the potato mixture.

In a separate bowl, combine the batter ingredients, adding the water gradually, and mix well. The batter needs to be just thick enough to coat the chillies.

Heat enough oil for deep-frying in a large, deep pan to 170°C (340°F) or until a cube of bread browns in 25 seconds when dropped into the oil. When the oil is hot enough, dip the stuffed chillies into the batter and carefully lower into the hot oil (you may need to work in batches). Cook for 4–5 minutes in total, turning them around halfway through, then remove with a slotted spoon to drain on kitchen paper.

Enjoy with your choice of chutney.

I can almost taste the sharpness of the raw Indian mango while I type up this recipe. The sourness of those mangoes is next level and it is perfect to beat any summer heat. In case you can't get hold of Indian mangoes, try to find the rock-hard green mangoes from supermarkets. They might not have the same level of sour, but you can add a squeeze of lime to intensify the flavour.

Aam ka salad | Mango slaw

SERVES 4

3 raw green Indian mangoes or 1 large raw green mango

1 red onion, thinly sliced

¼ teaspoon salt

¼ teaspoon ground cumin

½ teaspoon soft brown sugar

1 green chilli, finely chopped

Grate the mango of your choice, nice and thick. Mix this with the onion, salt, cumin, sugar and chillies, and serve.

Paneer is a firm favourite of my kids – they just love anything with it, and these crispy, delicious paneer fingers are a true winner. Easy to put together, you can prepare them ahead of time, place on a tray in the refrigerator and just fry them when ready to serve. These are great served with some Chilli Chutney.

Till paneer | Sesame seed paneer fingers

SERVES 4–6

500g (1lb 2oz) paneer
¼ teaspoon salt
¼ teaspoon chilli powder
¼ teaspoon chaat masala
¼ teaspoon ground turmeric
60g (2¼oz) panko breadcrumbs
70g (2½oz) sesame seeds
sunflower oil, for deep-frying
Chilli Chutney (see page 173), to serve

FOR THE BATTER

60g (2¼oz) plain flour
½ teaspoon salt
½ teaspoon chilli powder
½ teaspoon chaat masala
½ teaspoon ground turmeric
130ml (4¼fl oz) water

Cut the paneer into thin strips, about 5mm (¼ inch) thick. Mix the salt, chilli powder, chaat masala and ground turmeric in a small bowl. Sprinkle the mixture over the paneer strips, then turn and sprinkle the other sides too. Set aside.

In a separate bowl, mix together the flour, salt and all the spices for the batter. Add the water and whisk until you have a smooth batter.

In another bowl, mix together the breadcrumbs and sesame seeds.

Heat the oil for deep-frying in a large, deep pan to 170°C (340°F) or until a cube of bread browns in 25 seconds when dropped into the oil. When the oil is hot enough, dip the paneer strips into the batter, roll them in the breadcrumb mixture and gently lower them into the hot oil (you may need to cook them in batches). Cook for a minute on each side until lightly golden, then remove with a slotted spoon to drain on kitchen paper.

Serve immediately with some Chilli Chutney.

It was such a pleasure to visit Meena Aunty in her kitchen in Ahmedabad. Everything was so organised, from the utensils to the spices and the rest. She cooked an entire feast in minutes without even breaking a sweat. This delicious *palak muthiya* was my favourite of her dishes. Steaming the spinach with minimum flour and lots of gentle spices, then frying it to give it that crispness, gives amazing results.

Palak muthiya | Crispy spinach

SERVES 4

200g (7oz) chapatti flour

½ teaspoon ground turmeric

1 teaspoon ground coriander

1 teaspoon ground cumin

1 teaspoon salt

4 garlic cloves, grated

2.5cm (1 inch) piece of fresh root ginger, peeled and grated

¼ teaspoon bicarbonate of soda

1 tablespoon peanut oil

200g (7oz) spinach leaves, chopped

125ml (4fl oz) water

sea salt flakes, to garnish

Red Pepper Chutney (see page 162), to serve

FOR THE TADKA

3 tablespoons peanut oil

1 teaspoon mustard seeds

2 garlic cloves, finely chopped

2.5cm (1 inch) piece of fresh root ginger, peeled and finely chopped

Combine the flour, spices, salt, garlic, ginger and bicarbonate of soda in a bowl and mix well. Add the oil and rub it into the flour, then add the chopped spinach and water. Bring it all together and divide it into 4 equal portions. Shape them into thick sausages.

Bring a steamer pan to the boil, place the spinach sausages on the steamer tray, cover with the lid and steam over a medium heat for 20 minutes. Remove the spinach sausages (*muthiya*) from the steamer and set aside to cool. When cool, chop into slices, about 1cm (½ inch) thick.

For the tadka, heat the oil in a small pan and add the mustard seeds. Once they start to pop, add the garlic and ginger, and cook for 1 minute over a low heat. Add the pieces of *muthiya* and fry over a high heat for 2–4 minutes until the edges start to get crispy and golden.

Sprinkle with sea salt flakes and enjoy with some Red Pepper Chutney.

2 dried red chillies

1 bay leaf

1 black cardamom pod

4 green cardamom pods

1 teaspoon cumin seeds

2 teaspoons coriander seeds

1 blade of mace

2.5cm (1 inch) cinnamon stick

4 cloves

6 black peppercorns

1 teaspoon fennel seeds

½ teaspoon ground ginger

½ teaspoon black salt (kala namak)

FOR THE POHA

3 tablespoons sunflower oil

a pinch of asafoetida

30g (1oz) unsalted raw peanuts (with skins)

1 teaspoon cumin seeds

1 teaspoon mustard seeds

1 teaspoon fennel seeds

10 curry leaves

1 onion, finely chopped

250g (9oz) poha (flattened rice/beaten rice flakes – available online or in Indian grocery stores)

½ teaspoon salt

½ teaspoon ground turmeric

½ teaspoon caster sugar

juice of 1 lemon

You might have heard of the delicious *poha*, the perfect Indian breakfast, and the many ways of cooking it. *Poha* is flattened rice, used mainly to make snacks and light meals. This recipe is my take on the very popular Indoori poha, which as the name suggests comes from Indoor, a city in central India. The difference is that this *poha* is made with a particular spice mix called *jeeravan masala*. It is available as a readymade spice mix in Indoor, but we have to make it ourselves. Thankfully, it is really straightforward and so delicious that you can use it in other curries, or salads and soups too.

Indoori poha

Start by making the spice mix. Put all the spices, except the ground ginger and black salt, in a large pan and dry roast over a low heat for 2 minutes until fragrant and golden. Grind the roasted spices to a powder in a spice grinder, then pour into a bowl. Add the ground ginger and black salt, and mix together well.

Heat the oil in a saucepan over a medium heat and add the asafoetida and peanuts. Cook for 2 minutes until nicely golden, then add the cumin, mustard and fennel seeds. When they start to sizzle, add the curry leaves and onion, and cook for 5–6 minutes until softened and just beginning to get some colour.

Meanwhile, put the poha in a bowl and cover it with water. Mix it well, then immediately pass it through a sieve.

Add the salt, turmeric and sugar to the onion and mix well, then add the drained poha and mix again. Cover and cook over a low heat for 5 minutes.

Finally, add the lemon juice, mix well and plate up. Sprinkle the *jeervan masala* spice mix generously on top and serve straight away.

Store the leftover spice mix in a jar and use it when you next make poha.

These pakora are crunchy and super quick to prepare. If you are looking for a delicious snack, then this is the recipe for you. The peppers are the perfect size to form little rings and have a slight sweetness, which is a great match to the spices. Enjoy them with Coriander and Ginger Chutney.

Pepper pakora

SERVES 4

100g (3½oz) gram flour (besan)

50g (1¾oz) rice flour

1 teaspoon salt

1 teaspoon chilli powder

1 teaspoon ground coriander

1 teaspoon ground cumin

about 100ml (3½fl oz) water

sunflower oil, for deep-frying

3 sweet long peppers, sliced into 1cm (½ inch) rings

sea salt flakes, to garnish

Coriander and Ginger Chutney (see page 172), to serve (optional)

Put the flours, salt and spices into a bowl and slowly add enough water to form a thick batter.

Heat enough oil for deep-frying in a large, deep pan to 170°C (340°F) or until a cube of bread browns in 25 seconds when dropped into the oil. When the oil is hot enough, put the pepper slices into the batter and make sure they are all covered. Lower into the hot oil (in batches, if necessary) and fry for 2–3 minutes until crispy and golden. Remove with a slotted spoon to drain on kitchen paper.

Sprinkle with sea salt flakes and serve immediately with my Coriander and Ginger Chutney, if liked.

Methi gota is a popular snack in Gujarat and is often served as breakfast in restaurants there, too. I had it with a cup of chai and fell in love with it. Fenugreek is essential to this, so you will need to find some fresh leaves. The unique flavour comes from the slightly bitter fenugreek with all the spices, and the bicarbonate of soda gives it lightness. It's usually served with coriander chutney.

Methi gota | Fenugreek balls

SERVES 4

150ml (5fl oz) water

1 tablespoon peanut oil

½ teaspoon sugar

½ teaspoon salt

1 teaspoon ground coriander

1 teaspoon ground cumin

½ teaspoon ground turmeric

¼ teaspoon asafoetida

¼ teaspoon ground black pepper

2.5cm (1 inch) piece of fresh root ginger, peeled and grated

1 green chilli, finely chopped

¼ teaspoon bicarbonate of soda

10g (¼oz) fresh coriander leaves, finely chopped

60g (2¼oz) fresh fenugreek (leaves only), finely chopped

150g (5½oz) gram flour (besan)

sunflower oil, for frying

sea salt flakes, to garnish

Coriander and Ginger Chutney (see page 172), to serve (optional)

In a bowl, mix the water with the peanut oil, sugar, salt, spices, ginger, chilli and bicarbonate of soda, and stir well. Add the coriander and fenugreek leaves and mix together, then add the gram flour and mix until well combined.

Heat the oil for deep-frying in a large, deep pan to 170°C (340°F) or until a cube of bread browns in 25 seconds when dropped into the oil. When the oil is hot enough, take small, walnut-sized portions of the mixture and carefully lower into the oil. Reduce the heat to low for 2 minutes, then bring to 150°C (300°F) and cook for 4 more minutes, stirring often, until light brown and crispy. Remove with a slotted spoon to drain on kitchen paper.

Sprinkle with sea salt flakes and serve with Coriander and Ginger Chutney, if liked.

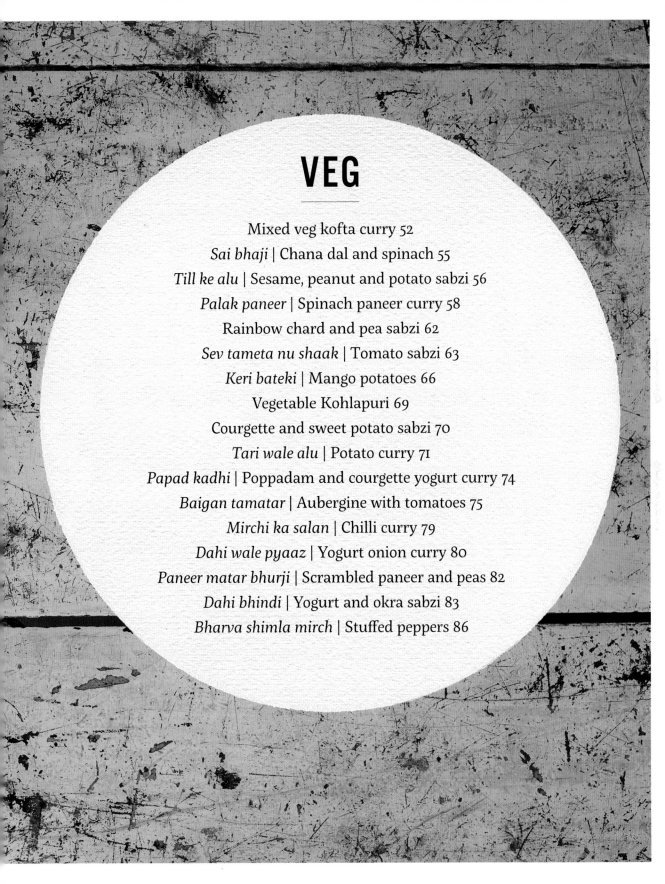

VEG

Mixed veg kofta curry 52

Sai bhaji | Chana dal and spinach 55

Till ke alu | Sesame, peanut and potato sabzi 56

Palak paneer | Spinach paneer curry 58

Rainbow chard and pea sabzi 62

Sev tameta nu shaak | Tomato sabzi 63

Keri bateki | Mango potatoes 66

Vegetable Kohlapuri 69

Courgette and sweet potato sabzi 70

Tari wale alu | Potato curry 71

Papad kadhi | Poppadam and courgette yogurt curry 74

Baigan tamatar | Aubergine with tomatoes 75

Mirchi ka salan | Chilli curry 79

Dahi wale pyaaz | Yogurt onion curry 80

Paneer matar bhurji | Scrambled paneer and peas 82

Dahi bhindi | Yogurt and okra sabzi 83

Bharva shimla mirch | Stuffed peppers 86

SERVES 4

FOR THE KOFTA

150g (5½oz) pointed cabbage, grated

1 carrot, grated

1 onion, finely chopped

2.5cm (1 inch) piece of fresh root ginger, peeled and grated

2 potatoes, boiled and mashed

10g (¼oz) fresh coriander, finely chopped

50g (1¾oz) gram flour (besan)

50g (1¾oz) cornflour

½ teaspoon salt

1 teaspoon garam masala

1 teaspoon ground cumin

1 teaspoon chilli powder

2 tablespoons sunflower oil, plus extra for deep-frying

FOR THE CURRY

3 tablespoons sunflower oil

4 cardamom pods

2 bay leaves

1 cinnamon stick

1 teaspoon cumin seeds

2 onions, blitzed or grated

2.5cm (1 inch) piece of fresh root ginger, peeled and grated

4 garlic cloves, grated

2 tomatoes, blitzed or grated

200ml (7fl oz) boiling water

½ teaspoon salt

½ teaspoon sugar

½ teaspoon chilli powder

½ teaspoon ground turmeric

1 teaspoon garam masala

1 teaspoon ground coriander

1 tablespoon dried fenugreek leaves (kasuri methi)

2 tablespoons double cream

The best thing about kofta curry is the versatility of the dish. I have shared kofta curries, such as paneer and potato kofta, in my books before, but these koftas contain a mixture of different vegetables. The particular combination of veg is what makes them special: crunchy cabbage and onion with sweet carrots and potato to help bind them together. They are perfect served on top of this simple curry, but I also highly recommend serving them on their own as a snack with a chutney at your next gathering or for a weekend meal.

Mixed veg kofta curry

For the kofta, first put all the veg in a large bowl and mix, then add the remaining ingredients and mix well. It's best to mash it by hand. Shape into 16 small, egg-shaped kofta.

Heat the oil for deep-frying in a large, deep pan to 170°C (340°F) or until a cube of bread browns in 25 seconds when dropped into the oil. When the oil is hot enough, fry the kofta a few at a time for 2–3 minutes until golden. Remove with a slotted spoon to drain on kitchen paper.

For the curry, heat the oil in a large pan, add the whole spices and let sizzle for a few seconds. Add the onions and cook over a low–medium heat for 8–10 minutes until deep golden. Add the ginger and garlic, and cook for 2 minutes before adding the tomatoes and boiling water. Cover and cook over a low heat for 15 minutes.

Add the salt, sugar and spices, and cook for a final 5 minutes. Add the cream and stir through. Serve the curry on a platter with the kofta placed on top.

I often make dal with spinach as it's a great combination and tastes amazing. But this is a new way of cooking the dal which I was introduced to by Bhumika. *Sai bhaji* is a very popular dish in the Sindhi culture, which is not surprising as it's delicious, creamy and also very healthy. Serve with *Koki* or any other roti.

Sai bhaji | Chana dal and spinach

SERVES 4

150g (5½oz) chana dal (split yellow peas)

1.4 litres (2½ pints) water

4 tablespoons peanut oil

1 teaspoon cumin seeds

4 garlic cloves, thinly sliced

2 medium onions, finely chopped

2 tomatoes, roughly chopped

400g (14 oz) spinach leaves, chopped

1 teaspoon salt

1 teaspoon ground turmeric

2 teaspoons ground coriander

1 teaspoon ground cumin

Koki (see page 117) or any other roti, to serve

Soak the chana dal in the water for 1 hour.

Heat the oil in a large pan and add the cumin seeds. Once they start to sizzle, add the garlic and cook for 1 minute over a low heat. Add the onions and cook for 5 minutes until softened, then add the tomatoes and cook for another 5 minutes until the tomatoes have started to soften. Add the spinach and cook for 2 minutes until wilted.

Add the soaked dal along with the soaking water, salt, turmeric and coriander. Cover and cook over a medium–low heat for 1 hour until the dal is cooked through and soft.

Finally, add the ground cumin and serve with your choice of roti.

This is a recipe I just had to make – inspired by a bit of Gujarati and a bit of Maharashtrian food, the sesame, peanut and potato sabzi is a must-try. If you are a potato fan, you will fall in love with this very simple dish which will be the star on your dinner table any time you serve it.

Till ke alu | Sesame, peanut and potato sabzi

SERVES 4

60g (2¼oz) unsalted raw peanuts (with skins)

4 tablespoons peanut oil

1 teaspoon cumin seeds

1 teaspoon mustard seeds

4 garlic cloves, thinly sliced

2.5cm (1 inch) piece of fresh root ginger, peeled and julienned

2 green chillies, thinly sliced

10 curry leaves

1 teaspoon salt

1 teaspoon ground turmeric

1 teaspoon mango powder (amchur)

1 teaspoon ground cumin

1 tablespoon sesame seeds

1 tablespoon jaggery

6 medium potatoes, boiled and cut into 2.5cm (1 inch) pieces

100ml (3½fl oz) boiling water

Dry roast the peanuts in a frying pan for 3–4 minutes over a low heat until golden and roasted well. Crush in a pestle and mortar to break them up.

In the same pan, heat the oil and add the cumin and mustard seeds. Let them sizzle for a minute, then add the garlic, ginger and chillies. After another minute, add the curry leaves followed by the salt, the spices, sesame seeds and jaggery. Add the cooked potatoes along with the boiling water, throw in the crushed peanuts and cook over a high heat for 5 minutes to get a few crispy corners.

Serve immediately.

I am aware that I have shared recipes for *palak paneer* in my previous books, but every so often you cook a recipe with variations and it turns into something extra special. I have always cooked this dish very simply, with salt, chilli and garlic, but this time I have cooked it in a style similar to what you find in restaurants in India. I hope you will love it! Great served with some flatbreads or rice.

Palak paneer | Spinach paneer curry

SERVES 4

400g (14 oz) fresh spinach

40g (1½oz) fresh coriander, roughly chopped

10g (¼oz) fresh mint, leaves only

200ml (7fl oz) water

2 tablespoons sunflower oil

1 teaspoon cumin seeds

4 garlic cloves, finely chopped

2.5cm (1 inch) piece of fresh root ginger, peeled and finely chopped

1 green chilli, finely chopped

2 medium onions, finely chppped

1 tomato, finely chopped

1 teaspoon chilli powder

1 teaspoon ground coriander

1 teaspoon ground cumin

1 teaspoon salt

400g (14oz) paneer, cubed

1 tablespoon dried fenugreek leaves (kasuri methi)

2 tablespoons double cream

1 tablespoon lemon juice

FOR THE TADKA

4 tablespoons ghee

4 garlic cloves, thinly sliced

1 teaspoon chilli flakes

Put the spinach, coriander and mint in a pan, pour in the water, then cover and cook for 5 minutes until wilted. Blitz to a purée in a food processor.

Heat the sunflower oil in a large pan and add the cumin seeds. Once they start to sizzle, add the garlic and ginger, and cook for a minute over a medium–low heat. Add the green chilli and onions and cook for 5–6 minutes until softened.

Reduce the heat to low, add the tomato and cook for 10 minutes.

Add the spices and salt, followed by the herby spinach purée, and cook for a further 5 minutes, then add the paneer and cook for 2 minutes. Stir in the dried fenugreek leaves, cream and lemon juice.

In a separate small pan, heat the ghee for the tadka, then add the garlic and cook for a minute until it starts to change colour. Remove from the heat and add the chilli flakes.

Pour the tadka over the *palak paneer* and serve.

I get locally grown rainbow chard in season and love a good *sabzi* – ample reasons for sharing this simple and delicious recipe. You can even cook it with kale if you like. Enjoy with a pile of rice.

Rainbow chard and pea sabzi

SERVES 4

3 tablespoons sunflower oil

¼ teaspoon asafoetida

1 teaspoon cumin seeds

2 onions, thinly sliced

200g (7oz) rainbow chard, chopped into 2.5cm (1 inch) pieces

½ teaspoon salt

½ teaspoon chilli powder

½ teaspoon ground turmeric

½ teaspoon garam masala

½ teaspoon ground coriander

200g (7oz) frozen peas

rice, to serve

Heat the oil in a pan over a medium heat and add the asafoetida and cumin seeds. Once they start to sizzle, add the onions and cook for 5 minutes until they start to soften. Now add the rainbow chard along with 2 tablespoons of water, cover and cook over a low–medium heat for 10 minutes.

Add the salt and all the spices and mix well, then stir in the frozen peas. Cook over a low heat for 5 minutes, then increase the heat to high and cook for a final 2 minutes. Serve immediately with rice.

When Renuka invited me to her home I expected a vegetarian feast, but I had no idea how quickly and with what ease she would cook it; in minutes, my plate was full of delicacies. I'd often eaten the famous Gujarati tomato sev with ready-made sev, but Renuka made fresh sev, which only took a few minutes, and added it directly to the curry. It was insanely delicious and made me wonder how such simple ingredients prepared with such little effort could taste so amazing. Enjoy with Bhakri or puri.

Sev tameta nu shaak | Tomato sabzi

SERVES 4

3 tablespoons peanut oil

¼ teaspoon asafoetida

1 teaspoon cumin seeds

8 tomatoes, finely chopped

1 teaspoon chilli powder

2 teaspoons ground cumin

2 teaspoons ground coriander

1 teaspoon ground turmeric

6 garlic cloves, finely chopped

400ml (14fl oz) water

1½ teaspoons jaggery, grated

1 teaspoon salt

a handful of fresh coriander leaves, finely chopped

Bhakri (see page 133) or puri (see pages 123 and 134), to serve

FOR THE SEV

140g (5oz) gram flour (besan), sieved

½ teaspoon salt

½ teaspoon ground turmeric

125ml (4fl oz) water

Heat the oil in a large pan and add the asafoetida followed by the cumin seeds. Once they start to sizzle, add the tomatoes, spices and garlic, and mix well. Add 100ml (3½fl oz) of the water and bring to the boil, then cover and cook over a medium heat for 5 minutes until the tomatoes have softened.

Add the jaggery along with the remaining 300ml (10fl oz) of water and mix well. Bring back to the boil and add the salt.

In a bowl prepare the sev batter, mixing the gram flour, salt and turmeric with the water to form a thick paste.

With the tomato curry at a boil, hold a slotted spoon over the pan. Pass the gram flour paste through the spoon, letting it drop directly into the curry. Use up all the sev paste and cook for 2–3 minutes over a medium heat until cooked through.

Sprinkle the curry with the chopped coriander and serve straight away with Bhakri or puri.

Keri means 'mango' and *bateki* means 'small potatoes'. You might make the mistake of thinking that this is going to taste sweet, but fear not – the mangoes used here are the small green Indian mangoes you can find in Asian stores. They are sharp and sour and just so lively. This recipe by Renuka is something she cooks for her family a lot during the summer season. It is a riot of flavours from the very sour mangoes with a touch of sweetness, to the spicy chilli – an unusual dish I fell in love with.

Keri bateki | Mango potatoes

SERVES 4

2 raw green Indian mangoes, grated

½ teaspoon salt

1 teaspoon soft brown sugar

a handful of fresh coriander leaves, finely chopped

750g (1lb 10oz) baby potatoes, peeled and boiled

FOR THE TADKA

2 tablespoons peanut oil

¼ teaspoon asafoetida

2 teaspoons chilli powder

Put the grated mangoes, salt, sugar and coriander in a bowl and mix well. Add the boiled potatoes while they are still hot and mix well.

In a small pan, heat the oil for the tadka and add the asafoetida. Once it sizzles, remove from the heat and add the chilli powder.

Pour the tadka over the mango potatoes, mix well and serve.

FOR THE SPICE BLEND

1 black cardamom pod

2 green cardamom pods

1 star anise

1 cinnamon stick

¼ teaspoon black peppercorns

1 teaspoon cumin seeds

1 teaspoon coriander seeds

1 tablespoon sesame seeds

4 dried red chillies

50g (1¾oz) fresh coconut, finely chopped

100ml (3½fl oz) water

FOR THE CURRY

20 cashew nuts

4 red dried chillies

100ml (3½fl oz) boiling water

4 tablespoons sunflower oil

¼ teaspoon asafoetida

1 onion, finely chopped

2 garlic cloves, finely chopped

2.5cm (1 inch) piece of fresh root ginger, peeled and finely chopped

400g (14oz) tin of chopped tomatoes, blitzed to a purée

200ml (7fl oz) water

1 tablespoon dried fenugreek leaves (kasuri methi)

1 teaspoon salt

1 teaspoon honey

4 tablespoons double cream

FOR THE VEG

4 tablespoons sunflower oil

1 green pepper, cut into 1cm (½ inch) dice

1 carrot, cut into 1cm (½ inch) dice

1 onion, cut into 1cm (½ inch) dice

100g (3½oz) frozen peas

200g (7oz) paneer, cubed

Vegetable Kolhapuri is a popular Maharashtrian dish which is commonly found on restaurant menus in India. Kolhapur is a town famous for its chillies and, although this might not be the original recipe (who knows what that one is), it is a dish that brings the flavours of spices and vegetables together in perfect harmony.

Vegetable Kohlapuri

Put all the spices for the blend in a pan and dry roast for 2 minutes until fragrant and starting to change colour. Remove to a bowl. In the same pan, dry roast the coconut for 2 minutes until lightly golden and fragrant. Once cooled down, add the coconut to the spices and blitz to a powder in a spice grinder or small food processor. Add the water to the powder and mix to a paste. Set aside.

For the curry, cover the cashew nuts and dried chillies with the boiling water and leave to soak for 15 minutes, then blitz to a paste. Set aside.

Heat the sunflower oil for the curry in a large pan over a medium heat and add the asafoetida. Once it starts to sizzle, add the onion and cook for 5 minutes until it softens. Add the garlic and ginger, cook for 1 minute, then stir in the cashew-chilli paste. Add the spice blend and mix well,

then add the puréed tomatoes along with the 200ml (7fl oz) water. Cook over a low heat for 15 minutes.

In a separate pan, prepare the veg. Heat the oil over a medium heat, add the pepper and carrot and cook for 5 minutes, then add the onion, peas and paneer, and cook for another 5 minutes. Add the cooked veg to the curry pan and cook for a further 5 minutes.

Finally, add the fenugreek leaves, salt, honey and cream to the curry and mix well. Serve immediately.

I love courgettes and they are in abundance in the summer. Although I particularly love them roasted, I like to eat them in many forms, whether in a salad, in curry or as koftas. Here I am using them in a super quick sabzi with sweet potato. The flavours bounce off each other and cumin is the spice that brings them together. Enjoy with some piping-hot Seeded Roti.

Courgette and sweet potato sabzi

SERVES 4

3 tablespoons sunflower oil

a pinch of asafoetida

1 teaspoon cumin seeds

1 large sweet potato, peeled and cut into wedges about 5cm (2 inches) long

2 courgettes, cut into batons about 5cm (2 inches) long

½ teaspoon salt

½ teaspoon chilli powder

1 teaspoon ground cumin

juice of ½ lime

Seeded Roti (see page 114), to serve

Heat the oil in a saucepan, then add the asafoetida followed by the cumin seeds. Once they start to sizzle, add the sweet potato wedges and cook over a medium–high heat for 5 minutes.

Add the courgettes along with 2 tablespoons of water, cover and cook for 5–8 minutes until the sweet potatoes are soft.

Add the salt, spices and lime juice, mix together well and serve with Seeded Roti.

These are the famous potatoes served with *Bedmi Puri* (see page 134). The flavours of the curry are a perfect match for the delicious *puri*. The small amount of gram flour here helps to give the curry a little bit of body and squashing the potato by hand helps it soak in all the flavours. If you can't serve it with piping hot *Bedmi Puri*, don't let that stop you from trying this – it's also great with *Masaledar Puri* (see page 123) or simply with a pile of rice.

SERVES 4

4 tablespoons sunflower oil

2 bay leaves

5 cardamom pods

5 cloves

1 teaspoon fennel seeds

1 teaspoon cumin seeds

2 green chillies, thinly sliced

¼ teaspoon asafoetida

1 teaspoon ground turmeric

1 teaspoon chilli powder

2 teaspoons ground coriander

1 tablespoon gram flour (besan)

4 tomatoes, blitzed to a purée

1 teaspoon salt

200ml (7fl oz) water

4 potatoes, boiled and cut into 2.5cm (1 inch) pieces

1 teaspoon garam masala

1 tablespoon dried fenugreek leaves (kasuri methi)

a handful of fresh coriander leaves, finely chopped

Bedmi Puri (see page 134), to serve

Tari wale alu | Potato curry

Heat the oil in a pan over a medium–low heat, add the bay leaves, cardamom and cloves, and give them a few seconds to sizzle. Add the fennel and cumin seeds, and let them sizzle for a few seconds before adding the green chillies and asafoetida.

Turn the heat to the lowest setting, then add the dry spices and then the gram flour, and cook for 2 minutes. Next add the tomato purée and salt, followed by the water. Cover and cook over a low–medium heat for 15 minutes.

Now squash the potato pieces by hand, add them to the curry and cook for 5 minutes. If you need more water at this stage, add another 200ml (7fl oz) of boiling water and cook for 5 minutes. Finally, stir in the garam masala, fenugreek leaves and coriander, and serve with *Bedmi Puri*.

When Meena Aunty cooked this *kadhi* for me she used homemade *vadi* and *papad*. But once I got back to the UK it was more difficult to find good-quality *vadi* (small balls made with cooked dried lentils, commonly used in Indian cooking). So I looked for good alternatives and finally settled on the combination of *papad* (poppadams) and courgettes, which went very well together. Serve with rice and Rotla or Bhakri.

Papad kadhi | Poppadam and courgette yogurt curry

In a large bowl, mix together the yogurt, gram flour, salt, turmeric, sugar and water, and whisk until smooth. Set aside.

Heat the oil in a large saucepan over a medium heat. Add the courgettes and cook for 6–8 minutes until golden, then remove with a slotted spoon to drain on kitchen paper. Spoon out the excess oil from the pan leaving only 2 tablespoons behind.

Reheat the oil in the pan and add the cumin seeds. Once they start to sizzle, add the garlic, ginger and green chilli, and cook for a minute, then add the yogurt mixture and cook over a low–medium heat for 15 minutes until it starts to thicken. Add the courgettes and papad along with the ground coriander and cumin, and cook for 10 minutes until the papad is cooked.

Sprinkle with the fresh coriander and serve with rice and breads.

SERVES 4

250g (9oz) natural yogurt

3 tablespoons gram flour (besan), sifted

1 teaspoon salt

1 teaspoon ground turmeric

½ teaspoon caster sugar

300ml (10fl oz) water

100ml (3½fl oz) sunflower oil

3 courgettes, halved lengthwise, then cut into 1cm (½ inch) slices

1 teaspoon cumin seeds

4 garlic cloves, finely chopped

1cm (½ inch) piece of fresh root ginger, peeled and finely chopped

1 green chilli, finely chopped

6 uncooked papad (uncooked poppadams, found in Asian stores), cut into 5cm (2 inch) pieces

½ teaspoon ground coriander

½ teaspoon ground cumin

a handful of fresh coriander, finely chopped

rice and Rotla (see page 139) or Bhakri (see page 133), to serve

For me, this is a new way of cooking aubergine –
keeping it simple and adding tons of flavours in a
single bowl, leaving you with just the cooking to do.
Enjoy this with absolutely anything, from Bhakri
(see page 133) to *puri*, rice or biryani (see page 148)
– go crazy!

Baigan tamatar | Aubergine with tomatoes

SERVES 2

2 onions, finely chopped

2.5cm (1 inch) piece of fresh root ginger, peeled and finely chopped

1 green chilli, finely chopped

a handful of fresh coriander, finely chopped

3 tablespoons peanut oil

3 tablespoons tomato purée

½ teaspoon salt

½ teaspoon ground turmeric

½ teaspoon chilli powder

1 large aubergine, sliced widthways into 5mm (¼ inch) discs

Put everything except the aubergine in a bowl and mix well. Add the aubergine slices and turn to coat well.

Heat a large frying pan over a high heat, pour everything in and cook for 5 minutes, then turn the aubergine over and cook for another 5 minutes. Reduce the heat to low and cook everything for a final 10 minutes, or until cooked through.

Serve warm or at room temperature.

Salan is a Hyderabadi curry made with a rich paste of peanuts, sesame seeds, coconut and gentle spicing. The little punch comes from the tamarind and the heat comes from the chillies. It is popularly served with biryani, but is great with some chapatti or parathas, too. Usually this curry is made with Bhavnagri chillies (which you can sometimes get in Asian stores). If they are not available, Thai chillies should do the job.

Mirchi ka salan | Chilli curry

SERVES 4

40g (1½oz) tamarind pulp

200ml (7fl oz) boiling water

6 tablespoons peanut oil

8 green chillies, slit lengthways

1 teaspoon cumin seeds

1 teaspoon mustard seeds

10 curry leaves

2 onions, finely chopped

1 teaspoon chilli powder

½ teaspoon ground turmeric

½ teaspoon garam masala

1 teaspoon ground cumin

FOR THE SPICE PASTE

70g (2½oz) unsalted raw peanuts (with skins)

3 tablespoons sesame seeds

1 tablespoon poppy seeds

¼ teaspoon fenugreek seeds

2 tablespoons desiccated coconut

4 garlic cloves, roughly chopped

2.5cm (1 inch) piece of fresh root ginger, peeled and roughly chopped

50ml (2fl oz) water

Start with the spice paste. Dry roast the peanuts for 5 minutes until fragrant and golden. Remove them to a food processor. In the same pan, dry roast the sesame and poppy seeds for 2 minutes until golden and transfer to the food processor. Finally, dry roast the fenugreek seeds for 2 minutes, then add the coconut and cook for another 2 minutes. Add to the food processor along with the garlic, ginger and water. Blitz to a paste.

Soak the tamarind pulp in the boiling water for 15 minutes.

Meanwhile, heat the oil in a pan and fry the green chillies for 2 minutes. Remove with a slotted spoon to a plate.

Add the cumin and mustard seeds to the same pan and let sizzle. Add the curry leaves, then the onions and cook for 6–8 minutes until golden. Add the ground spices and then the spice paste.

Strain the tamarind mixture through a sieve into a bowl, squeezing the pulp to extract as much flavour as possible. Add the tamarind water to the pan along with an extra 200ml (7fl oz) of water and the green chillies. Cover and cook for 15 minutes, then serve.

Onions are the one thing I would find very difficult to ever give up, as I use a lot of them in my cooking. So, this curry is like heaven to me – a curry made with just onions, magical! There is so much flavour with all the spices, and the yogurt brings delicacy. Try it with some Bhakri (see page 133) or parathas (see page 117, 121 or 128).

Dahi wale pyaaz | Yogurt onion curry

SERVES 4

1 tablespoon fennel seeds

1 tablespoon coriander seeds

2 teaspoons cumin seeds

4 tablespoons sunflower oil

¼ teaspoon asafoetida

2 dried red chillies

400g (14oz) tin of chopped tomatoes, blitzed to a purée

200ml (7fl oz) water

½ teaspoon salt

½ teaspoon ground turmeric

1 teaspoon chilli powder

4 tablespoons natural yogurt

600g (1lb 5oz) shallots, peeled

In a large pan, dry roast the fennel, coriander and 1 teaspoon of the cumin seeds for 2 minutes until fragrant and starting to change colour. Transfer to a pestle and mortar and crush to a powder. Set aside.

Heat the oil in the same pan over a medium heat, add the remaining teaspoon of cumin seeds and the asafoetida, and let sizzle. Next, add the red chillies and, after a few seconds, add the puréed tomatoes and half the water. Cover and cook for 5 minutes. Add the crushed spices, salt, turmeric and chilli powder and cook for a minute, then remove from the heat.

Add the yogurt with the remaining water and mix through, then return the pan to a low heat and cook for 2 minutes. Add the shallots, cover and cook over a low–medium heat for 20–25 minutes until the shallots are almost translucent. Stir after 5 minutes to stop the shallots from catching. Uncover and cook for a final minute before serving.

Bhurji means 'scrambled' in Hindi and this is a great scrambled paneer and peas, with simple and delicious flavours. Anything with paneer is always a hit in my house. This is one of those dishes that my mum would prepare to eat with crispy hot parathas, and now I make it often as a quick dinner and serve with whatever flatbread I might have to hand. This also goes really well with some dal and rice.

Paneer matar bhurji | Scrambled paneer and peas

SERVES 4

2 tablespoons sunflower oil

1 teaspoon mustard seeds

1 onion, finely chopped

1 green chilli, finely chopped

2.5cm (1 inch) piece of fresh root ginger, peeled and grated

2 tomatoes, finely chopped

1 teaspoon salt

1 teaspoon ground turmeric

1 teaspoon chilli powder

1 teaspoon ground cumin

1 teaspoon amchur (mango powder)

450g (1lb) paneer, crumbled or grated

100g (3½oz) frozen peas

a handful of fresh coriander, finely chopped

your choice of flatbread, to serve

Heat the oil in a saucepan and add the mustard seeds. When they start to sizzle, add the onion and chilli, and cook for 5–6 minutes over a medium heat until softened and beginning to change colour. Add the ginger and cook for another minute.

Add the chopped tomatoes, cover and cook for 5 minutes until softened.

Add the salt and spices and mix well. Add the crumbled or grated paneer and peas, mix well, then cover and cook over a low heat for 5 minutes.

Sprinkle the fresh coriander on top and serve with your choice of flatbread.

Okra (*bhindi*) is tricky – like Marmite, you either love it or hate it. But I think the people who hate it have not tried cooking it the right way. You should never wash okra after cutting, always before; dry it well and then start to chop and cook, ensuring you cook out the sliminess. With these tips in mind, try this simple yet punchy *dahi bhindi*. With the basic spices and a bit of creamy yogurt, this is one to enjoy with some Seeded Roti (see page 114), *puri*, Bhakri (see page 133) or *Thepla* (see page 135).

Dahi bhindi | Yogurt and okra sabzi

SERVES 4

4 tablespoons sunflower oil

500g (1lb 2oz) okra, halved lengthways

½ teaspoon salt

¼ teaspoon asafoetida

1 teaspoon mustard seeds

2 medium onions, thinly sliced

½ teaspoon chilli powder

½ teaspoon ground turmeric

½ teaspoon garam masala

½ teaspoon ground coriander

100g (3½oz) natural yogurt

50ml (2fl oz) water

your choice of flatbread, to serve

Heat 2½ tablespoons of the oil in a pan and add the okra with the salt. Cook over a medium heat for 10 minutes until the sliminess has gone and the okra are golden. Remove from the pan and set aside.

Add the remaining oil to the pan. Once hot, add the asafoetida and then the mustard seeds. Once they start to sizzle, add the onions and cook for 7–8 minutes until golden. Now add the spices and remove from the heat. Add the yogurt and water and stir through, then return to a low heat and cook for 5 minutes.

Add the okra back to the pan and cook for a final 5 minutes until most of the liquid has gone.

Serve with your choice of flatbread.

The slight sweetness and crunch of the peppers with the soft spicy potato filling makes this a great snack, or a side with your meal. Team it up with some dal or enjoy it with pulao. You can even make it with green and yellow peppers to mix it up a bit.

Bharva shimla mirch | Stuffed peppers

SERVES 4

3 medium potatoes, boiled and mashed

½ teaspoon salt

½ teaspoon chilli powder

½ teaspoon chaat masala, plus extra to serve

a handful of fresh coriander, finely chopped

2 red peppers

100ml (3½fl oz) sunflower oil

Put the mashed potatoes in a bowl with the salt, spices and coriander, and mix well.

With a sharp knife, make a hole in each pepper from the top taking off the stem and removing the core and seeds. Stuff the peppers with the potato mixture quite tightly. Carefully slice the stuffed peppers into rings, 1cm (½ inch) thick, making sure the potato filling stays inside each ring.

Heat the oil in a large, deep frying pan. Once hot, carefully place the stuffed pepper rings in the pan and cook for 2–3 minutes on each side until golden.

Sprinkle some extra chaat masala on top and serve.

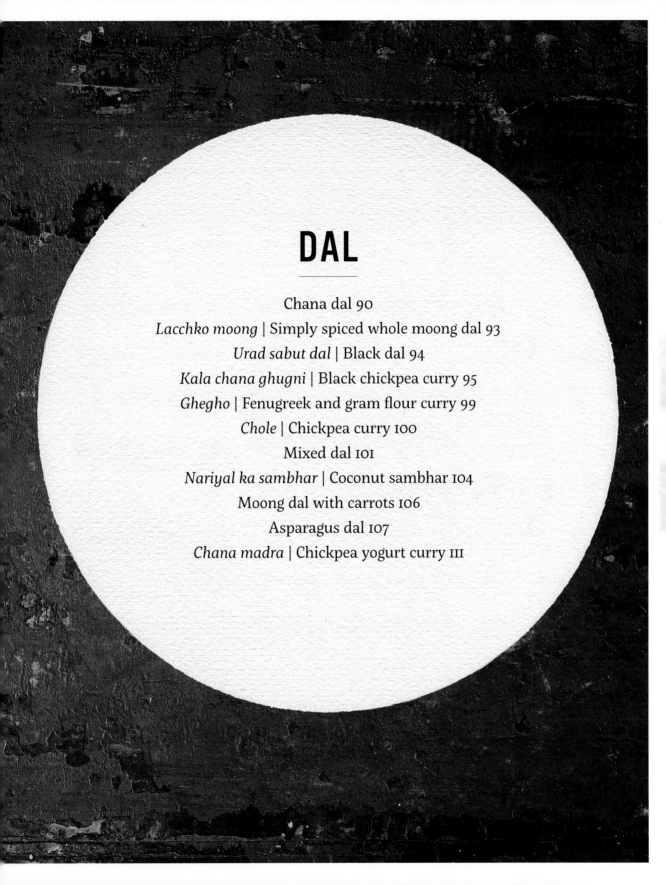

DAL

Chana dal 90

Lacchko moong | Simply spiced whole moong dal 93

Urad sabut dal | Black dal 94

Kala chana ghugni | Black chickpea curry 95

Ghegho | Fenugreek and gram flour curry 99

Chole | Chickpea curry 100

Mixed dal 101

Nariyal ka sambhar | Coconut sambhar 104

Moong dal with carrots 106

Asparagus dal 107

Chana madra | Chickpea yogurt curry 111

This chana dal is one half of the famous Sindhi breakfast dish *dal pakwaan*, which is a match made in heaven – the combination of creamy chana dal with crispy *pakwaan* bread is unbeatable. This is a family recipe of Bhumika, who lovingly cooked it for me in her beautiful kitchen in Gujarat. Once I started eating it, I found it hard to stop. Served with some Coriander and Ginger Chutney or Tamarind Chutney, it's an unforgettable feast. You can prepare all the elements of this meal beforehand – dal, *Pakwaan* and chutneys – and assemble it just before serving.

Chana dal

SERVES 4

250g (9oz) chana dal (split yellow peas)

50g (1¾oz) moong dal (split mung beans)

1.2 litres (2 pints) water

1 teaspoon salt

1 teaspoon ground turmeric

1 tomato, chopped

1 teaspoon chilli powder

1 teaspoon amchur (mango powder)

FOR THE TADKA

2 tablespoons peanut oil

1 teaspoon cumin seeds

a handful of fresh coriander leaves, finely chopped

TO SERVE

Pakwaan (see page 122)

Coriander and Ginger Chutney (see page 172) or Tamarind Chutney (see page 179)

chopped red onions

fresh coriander (optional)

Put the dals, water, salt, turmeric and tomato in a large pan and bring to the boil. Reduce to a simmer and cook for 1 hour over a medium–low heat until the dal is soft and cooked through. Remove from the heat, add the chilli powder and amchur, and let it sit for 10 minutes.

To prepare the tadka, heat the oil in a small pan and add the cumin seeds. Once they start to sizzle, remove from the heat and add the chopped coriander.

Immediately pour the tadka over the cooked dal and serve with *Pakwaan*, your choice of chutney, chopped red onions and fresh coriander, if liked.

This is a recipe taught to me by Avani, who was so warm and welcoming. She invited me into her kitchen and cooked a fabulous vegetarian feast. This *lacchko moong* is something she cooks often for her family. The reason for soaking the dal is that it makes it quicker to cook. If you don't have time to soak, just cook it for longer (40–45 minutes). I love the simplicity of this dal – no frills, just focussed on the beans with basic spices.

Lacchko moong | Simply spiced whole moong dal

SERVES 4

300g (10½oz) whole moong dal (mung beans)

1.5 litres (2¾ pints) warm water

4 tablespoons peanut oil

1 teaspoon mustard seeds

2 green chillies, thinly sliced

¼ teaspoon asafoetida

1 teaspoon ground turmeric

1 teaspoon ground cumin

1 teaspoon salt

1 tablespoon jaggery, grated

juice of ½ lime

Soak the dal in the warm water in a large saucepan for 1 hour. Alternatively, you can soak it overnight in cold water.

Bring the dal to a boil and cook for 30–35 minutes until the dal is soft, cooked through and has absorbed most of the water.

Heat the peanut oil in a separate large pan and add the mustard seeds, chillies and asafoetida. Once they start to sizzle, add the spices, salt and jaggery along with the cooked dal and mix well. Stir in the lime juice and serve.

Rich, creamy and delicious, this is one of my favourite dals to cook when I have a bit of time on my hands. Its simplicity of flavours and natural creaminess is what makes it so special. Try it with Seeded Roti, *Bati* or Bhakri; the choice is yours.

Urad sabut dal | Black dal

SERVES 4

300g (10½oz) whole urad dal (black lentils)

1 litre (1¾ pints) water

1½ teaspoons salt

4 tablespoons ghee

1 teaspoon cumin seeds

1 onion, finely chopped

4 garlic cloves, finely chopped

2 tablespoons tomato purée

1 teaspoon chilli powder

1 teaspoon garam masala

Seeded Roti (see page 114), Bati (see page 116) or Bhakri (see page 133), to serve

In a large saucepan, soak the dal in the water overnight or for at least 6 hours.

When ready to cook, bring the soaked dal to the boil, add the salt, then reduce to a simmer and cook for 1 hour. By this time, the water should have been absorbed. Add another 1 litre (1¾ pints) of boiling water to the pan and continue to cook for another 30 minutes until the dal is fully cooked and soft.

Heat the ghee in a separate large pan over a medium heat and add the cumin seeds. Once they start to sizzle, add the onion and cook for 6–8 minutes until golden. Add the garlic and cook for another minute, then add the tomato purée along with a couple of tablespoons of water and cook for 5 minutes.

Add the cooked dal to the pan along with the chilli powder and garam masala. Cook for 10 minutes, then add another 500ml (18fl oz) of water, if needed. Let sit for 15 minutes before serving with your choice of accompaniment.

I have always known *ghugni* to be a Bengali curry made with white peas – it is delicious; but recently I came across this version from Bihar made with black chickpeas. A popular dish in households across that state, this can be cooked in several ways. If you use a pressure cooker or instant pot it is ready in minutes, but it takes time to cook in a pan. However, it's well worth all the effort. This is great as a snack or as a main served with rice or *Masaledar Puri*.

Kala chana ghugni | Black chickpea curry

SERVES 4

300g (10½oz) black chickpeas (kala chana)

2 litres (3½ pints) water

½ teaspoon black peppercorns

1 teaspoon cumin seeds

1 green chilli, chopped

2.5cm (1 inch) piece of fresh root ginger, peeled and roughly chopped

4 garlic cloves, chopped

4 tablespoons sunflower oil

2 medium onions, finely chopped

1 teaspoon chilli powder

2 teaspoons ground coriander

1 teaspoon caster sugar

salt

rice or *Masaledar Puri* (see page 123), to serve (optional)

TO GARNISH

sliced red onions

a handful of fresh coriander, finely chopped

Soak the chickpeas in the water in a large saucepan for at least 6 hours or overnight.

Bring the soaked chickpeas to the boil, then cook over a medium heat for 1 hour.

Crush the peppercorns, cumin seeds, green chilli, ginger and garlic with a pinch of salt in a pestle and mortar.

Heat the oil in a pan over a medium heat, add the crushed paste and cook for a minute, then add the onions and cook for 6–8 minutes until golden. Add the spices, sugar and 2 teaspoons of salt, then add the chickpeas along with 200ml (7fl oz) of boiling water. Cover and cook for another 30–40 minutes over a medium heat until the chickpeas are soft and cooked through.

Garnish with sliced red onions and chopped coriander and serve with some steaming hot rice or *Masaledar Puri*, if liked.

When Avani told me about this dish, I thought she was going to make a *kadhi*, which is also a gram flour curry, but this is something so different to anything I had tried before. The slightly bitter flavour of fenugreek that I love matched with the earthiness of the gram flour and basic spices is simply phenomenal. A refreshing, light curry to serve with Bhakri (see page 133) or Rotla (see page 139).

Ghegho | Fenugreek and gram flour curry

SERVES 4

4 tablespoons peanut oil

¼ teaspoon asafoetida

150g (5½oz) fresh fenugreek, leaves picked and chopped

½ teaspoon ground turmeric

½ teaspoon chilli powder

1 teaspoon ground coriander

125g (4½oz) gram flour (besan)

1 litre (1¾ pints) water

1 tablespoon jaggery

Heat the oil in a large pan over a medium heat and add the asafoetida. Once it starts to sizzle, add the fenugreek leaves followed by the spices and cook for 1 minute.

Mix the gram flour into the water and whisk to smoothen. Add this to the fenugreek pan and stir for a minute, then cook over a low heat for around 20 minutes until the watery mix has thickened and become more like pancake batter in consistency. Add the jaggery and cook for another minute, then serve.

SERVES 4

FOR THE CHICKPEAS

400g (14oz) dried chickpeas

1.6 litres (scant 3 pints) water

1 teaspoon salt

1 dried red chilli

2 black cardamom pods

1 bay leaf

2 strong black tea bags

1 teaspoon bicarbonate of soda

50g (1¾oz) tamarind pulp

100ml (3½fl oz) boiling water

2.5cm (1 inch) piece of fresh root ginger, peeled and finely chopped

FOR THE SPICE BLEND

2 black cardamom pods

10 black peppercorns

2 green cardamom pods

1 blade of mace

1 teaspoon dried fenugreek leaves (kasuri methi)

1 star anise

2 cloves

½ teaspoon ground cinnamon

½ teaspoon chilli powder

½ teaspoon ground cumin

1 tablespoon ground coriander

TO SERVE

red onion rings

2.5cm (1 inch) piece of fresh root ginger, peeled and julienned

2 tablespoons salted butter

Bhatura (see page 129)

This is proper Punjabi *chole* which is served alongside Bhatura. An intense chickpea curry with no onion and no tomatoes, its flavours come from the spices and the chickpeas themselves. The classic combination of *chole bhatura* will make any occasion special – I'm sure you will love it.

Chole | Chickpea curry

In a large saucepan, soak the chickpeas in the water overnight. The next day, add all the other chickpea ingredients, aside from the tamarind, boiling water and ginger, to the pan, bring to the boil, then cover and cook for 30 minutes until beginning to soften.

Meanwhile, soak the tamarind pulp in the boiling water for 10–15 minutes, then strain it through a sieve into a bowl, squeezing the pulp to extract as much flavour as possible. Set the tamarind water aside.

For the spice blend, heat a dry frying pan over a low heat, add the whole spices and dry roast for 2 minutes, then add all the powdered spices. Remove from the heat and blitz it all to a smooth powder in a spice grinder.

Add the spice blend to the cooking chickpeas along with the tamarind water and the finely chopped ginger. Cook for another 30 minutes until the chickpeas are so soft they start to break up. If the mixture starts to dry out, add another 200ml (7fl oz) of boiling water while cooking. Remove the tea bags.

Serve with the red onion rings, julienned ginger and butter on top, accompanied by Bhatura.

Dal bati is a very popular dish you can find in many regions in India like Rajasthan, Madhya Pradesh and Gujarat. This dish is made with a combination of a few different lentils, which is what gives it that creamy texture and earthy flavour. Finished with a vibrant *tadka*, it is served with *Bati* – simply put, bread dough balls that are cooked and dunked in ghee. With a side of Churma (see page 204), this is a dish you don't want to miss. You can even enjoy this dal with just some rice or chapatti.

Mixed dal

Soak all the dal in the water in a large saucepan for 2 hours, then bring to the boil over a medium heat. Add the salt, turmeric and ghee, reduce to a simmer and cook for 30–40 minutes until the lentils are cooked through and break open, making the mixture thick.

In another pan, make the tadka. Heat the ghee, add the asafoetida and cumin seeds and let them sizzle. Now add the dried red chillies with the garlic, ginger and green chilli. Cook for a minute, then add the onion and cook for 6–8 minutes until golden. Add the tomato and cook for 10 minutes until softened. Add the spices and salt and mix well, then add the coriander and the cooked lentils. At this stage, add 100–200ml (3½–7fl oz) of boiling water, if needed.

Serve hot with piping hot *Bati* alongside.

SERVES 4

100g (3½oz) toor dal (split pigeon peas)

100g (3½oz) chana dal (split yellow peas)

100g (3½oz) whole moong dal (mung beans)

50g (1¾oz) red lentils (masoor dal)

1.5 litres (2¾ pints) water

1 teaspoon salt

1 teaspoon ground turmeric

1 teaspoon ghee

Bati (see page 116), to serve

FOR THE TADKA

4 tablespoons ghee

¼ teaspoon asafoetida

1 teaspoon cumin seeds

2 dried red chillies

4 garlic cloves, finely chopped

2.5cm (1 inch) piece of fresh root ginger, peeled and finely chopped

1 green chilli, finely chopped

1 onion, finely chopped

1 tomato, finely chopped

½ teaspoon ground turmeric

½ teaspoon chilli powder

2 teaspoons ground coriander

½ teaspoon salt

a handful of fresh coriander, finely chopped

SERVES 4

3 tablespoons sunflower oil

1 teaspoon mustard seeds

10–12 shallots, halved

4 drumsticks (moringa pods), strings removed, cut into 7.5cm (3 inch) pieces

½ teaspoon salt

½ teaspoon ground turmeric

rice, to serve (optional)

FOR THE TAMARIND WATER

50g (1¾oz) tamarind pulp

200ml (7fl oz) boiling water

FOR THE PASTE

2 tablespoons sunflower oil

2 dried red chillies

2 teaspoons chana dal (split yellow peas)

2 teaspoons coriander seeds

¼ teaspoon fenugreek seeds

¼ teaspoon asafoetida

80g (3oz) fresh coconut, roughly chopped

200ml (7fl oz) water

FOR THE DAL

200g (7oz) toor dal (split pigeon peas)

1.4 litres (2½ pints) water

1 teaspoon salt

1 teaspoon ground turmeric

FOR THE TADKA

2 tablespoons sunflower oil

1 teaspoon mustard seeds

10 curry leaves

2 dried red chillies

Sambhar is a lentil dish prepared in the south of India and all regions have their own versions. I went to visit my college friend Lakshmi in Mumbai after 10 years and she kindly invited me over to her parents' house where her mum cooked me a vegetarian feast. There was everything from *sambhar* and chutneys to *rasam* (soup), rice, *dosa* and also a dessert. I am a big fan of onions, so this *sambhar*, served on a pile of piping hot rice, was my favourite. I was in heaven.

Nariyal ka sambhar | Coconut sambhar

To make the tamarind water, soak the tamarind pulp in the boiling water for 10–15 minutes, then strain it through a sieve into a bowl, squeezing the pulp to extract as much flavour as possible. Set the tamarind water aside.

Next make the paste. Heat the oil in a pan over a low heat, add the chillies, chana dal and coriander seeds and cook for 1 minute before adding the fenugreek seeds and asafoetida. Cook for a further minute, then add the coconut and cook for another minute. Remove from the heat and let it cool slightly, then add the water and blitz to a paste in a food processor.

In the same pan, heat the oil and add the mustard seeds. Once they start to sizzle, add the shallots and cook for 5 minutes until they start to soften. Add the drumsticks and the tamarind water with an additional 200ml (7fl oz)

of water, then add the salt and turmeric, cover and cook for 10 minutes.

Meanwhile, start cooking the dal with the water, salt and turmeric. Bring to the boil, then reduce to a simmer and cook for 30 minutes until softened.

Add the dal to the shallot pan, cover and cook for a further 10 minutes.

Heat the oil for the tadka in a small pan and add the mustard seeds, curry leaves and chillies. Let it sizzle for a few seconds, then pour over the *sambhar*. Enjoy with a pile of piping hot rice, if liked.

This is one of the dals I make very often in the week. Not only is it ready in minutes, I also love that it is super healthy and everyone in the family enjoys it equally. Serve it with plain rice or Rotla or any other flatbread of your choice. Or, if you don't want any accompaniment, simply enjoy it as a soup.

Moong dal with carrots

SERVES 4

200g (7oz) moong dal
(split mung beans)

1 litre (1¾ pints) water

1 teaspoon salt

1 teaspoon ground turmeric

2 carrots, grated

rice, Rotla (see page 139)
or your choice of flatbread,
to serve

FOR THE TADKA

4 tablespoons ghee

1 teaspoon cumin seeds

4 garlic cloves, thinly sliced

a handful of fresh coriander,
finely chopped

1 teaspoon chilli powder

Put the dal, water, salt, turmeric and grated carrots into a saucepan and bring to the boil. Cover and cook over a low–medium heat for 15 minutes until cooked and soft.

Heat the ghee in a separate small pan and add the cumin seeds. Once they start to sizzle, add the garlic and cook over a low heat for 1 minute until lightly golden. Remove from the heat, add the coriander and chilli powder, then pour over the cooked dal. Serve with rice, Rotla or your choice of flatbread.

There is no particular reason for this recipe to appear here other than that I love asparagus. It grows locally to me and I like to use it in Indian dishes to make the most of its season. This dal recipe is easy and lets the asparagus shine equally with the toor dal, making it completely delicious. Serve with some rice or roti of any kind. You can also enjoy it just as soup.

Asparagus dal

SERVES 4

250g (9oz) toor dal (split pigeon peas)

½ teaspoon salt

½ teaspoon ground turmeric

1.2 litres (2 pints) water

4 tablespoons ghee

1 teaspoon cumin seeds

20 asparagus stems, woody parts removed, halved

4 garlic cloves, thinly sliced

1 tablespoon chilli oil

rice or roti, to serve (optional)

Put the toor dal, salt, turmeric and water in a pan, bring to the boil, then reduce to a simmer, partly cover and cook for 30 minutes until the dal is cooked through and soft.

In another pan, heat the ghee and add the cumin seeds. Once the seeds start to sizzle, add the asparagus and cook over a low heat for 10 minutes. Now add the garlic and cook for another 2 minutes. Finally, add the cooked dal to the pan, drizzle the chilli oil on top and serve with rice or roti, if liked.

Very different to the usual Punjabi *chole* that
I make all the time, in this recipe the chickpeas
are cooked with yogurt and spices making the dish
refreshingly light. This popular *chana madra* is
from the Himachal region of India, where it is made
for all sorts of occasions, festivals and weddings.
Serve with some piping hot rice, if liked.

Chana madra | Chickpea yogurt curry

SERVES 4

FOR THE YOGURT

300ml (10fl oz) natural
yogurt

1 teaspoon chilli powder

1 teaspoon ground turmeric

1 teaspoon salt

1 teaspoon ground coriander

FOR THE CURRY

4 tablespoons ghee

1 teaspoon cumin seeds

¼ teaspoon asafoetida

2 bay leaves

4 cloves

4 black peppercorns

1 black cardamom pod

1 blade of mace

2 dried red chillies

2 green chillies, chopped

2 × 400g (14oz) tins of
chickpeas, drained

In a bowl, mix the yogurt and spices. Set aside.

For the curry, heat the ghee in a large pan, add the
cumin seeds and asafoetida, and let sizzle for a few
seconds. Next, add all the spices and the chillies and
mix well. Remove from the heat, add the spiced
yogurt and stir continuously for a few seconds, then
return to a low heat and cook for 2 minutes. Add the
chickpeas and cook for a final 10 minutes, then serve.

FLATBREADS

Seeded roti 114

Bati | Baked dough balls 116

Koki | Onion paratha 117

Palak paneer paratha | Spinach and paneer paratha 121

Pakwaan | Crispy pastries 122

Masaledar puri | Spiced-up puri 123

Instant rice dosa 126

Sattu paratha | Gram flour-stuffed paratha 128

Bhatura 129

Bhakri 133

Bedmi puri | Dal-stuffed puri 134

Thepla | Fenugreek flatbreads 135

Rotla 139

A piping hot roti or chapatti is not just great with any *sabzi* or curry but also heavenly on its own. This roti is soft on the inside but has a slightly crunchy layer on the outside with a mixture of seeds, which taste amazing with the turmeric-flavoured dough.

Seeded roti

MAKES 10

300g (10½oz) chapatti flour, plus extra for dusting

½ teaspoon salt

½ teaspoon ground turmeric

about 150ml (5fl oz) water

150g (5½oz) mixed seeds, such as sunflower, sesame, pumpkin and flaxseeds

butter or ghee, to serve

Put the flour, salt and turmeric in a large bowl and mix well. Now add the water a little at a time until you have a soft dough. You might need a little bit more or less water. Knead for 2 minutes, then cover and leave to rest for 10 minutes.

Divide the dough into 10 equal portions and shape them into balls. Put the mixed seeds in a bowl. Take one ball at a time and press the dough into the seeds, then roll it out on a flour-dusted work surface to a disc, 13–15cm (5–6 inches) in diameter.

Heat a dry skillet or flat frying pan over a medium heat. Once it is hot, cook each roti for a minute on each side, pressing gently on the borders of the roti to encourage it to puff up. Spread some butter or ghee on top of each roti and serve.

Dal bati is a Rajasthani delicacy made for special occasions, such as Diwali and weddings. The Mixed Dal is made with a combination of lentils and the *bati* (bread rolls) are made with wholewheat flour and traditionally cooked over a cow-dung-fuelled fire. The history of *bati* is fascinating – it is believed to have been a wartime meal for soldiers who would break up the dough and leave it to cook under a thin layer of sand in the sun. My mum still cooks *bati* over cow dung, which adds to the flavour. Here I cook them in the oven and on the stove top, but they are great cooked on a barbecue too. Don't skip soaking them in ghee, as it is a crucial step.

Bati | Baked dough balls

MAKES 12

250g (9oz) chapatti flour

50g (1¾oz) fine semolina

½ teaspoon salt

½ teaspoon baking powder

½ teaspoon carom seeds

3 tablespoons ghee, plus 150g (5½oz) for frying

160ml (5½fl oz) water

Mixed Dal (see page 101), to serve

Preheat the oven to 180°C (350°F), Gas Mark 4. Line a baking tray with some baking paper.

Put the flour and semolina in a large bowl and add the salt, baking powder, carom seeds and the 3 tablespoons of ghee. Rub the ghee into the rest of the ingredients, then add the water a little at a time to make a soft dough. You might not need all the water or you may need a bit more. Knead for a minute, cover and leave to rest for 15 minutes.

Divide the rested dough into 12 equal portions and roll them into balls. Make a cross cut on top of each with a sharp knife and press each ball gently to slightly flatten the top. Place on the prepared baking tray and bake for 20 minutes.

Heat a dry skillet or flat frying pan over a high heat until hot. Remove the *bati* from the oven and place straight onto the hot pan. Cook for 2 minutes on each side until the surface turns brown. Now pour over the ghee for frying and cook for a minute more on each side.

Serve the *bati* hot with Mixed Dal.

During my visit to Gujarat I was introduced to Bhumika, who has moved with her husband to the outskirts of Ahmedabad and built a lovely small kitchen garden. Being a vegetarian and a Sindhi, she is very passionate about keeping her family recipes alive, and *koki* is one of them. A simple paratha that is packed with flavour with the addition of just a handful of ingredients. It has a unique design on it which helps it cook through and adds to the charm.

Koki | Onion paratha

MAKES 10

300g (10½oz) chapatti flour, plus extra for dusting

1 onion, finely chopped

1 green chilli, finely chopped

a handful of fresh coriander, finely chopped

1 teaspoon salt

1 teaspoon anardana (pomegranate) powder

2 tablespoons peanut oil, plus extra for cooking

160ml (5½fl oz) water

Tomato Chutney (see page 166), to serve (optional)

Put all the ingredients except the water in a bowl and then slowly add the water a little at a time to make a slightly hard dough. You might not need all the water or may need a bit more. You don't need to rest this dough, as resting it will make it too soft with all the onions in it. Once the dough is ready, make the *kokis* straight away.

Divide the dough into 10 equal portions. Roll each portion out on a flour-dusted work surface into a disc, roughly 13–15cm (5–6 inches) in diameter with rough edges. Take a knife and gently score lines all over the surface of the dough, cross-hatched to create diamond shapes. Don't cut all the way through.

Heat a dry skillet or flat frying pan over a hot heat. Cook each bread for 2–3 minutes, then add 1 teaspoon of oil to each side and continue to cook, turning as needed, until golden and crispy.

Serve hot with my Tomato Chutney.

Paratha has many variations. This recipe is one I came up with to keep my kids happy. They love *palak paneer* (spinach and paneer curry), so I decided to give it the shape of a paratha, adding spinach to the dough and paneer as a filling. The result is this winning recipe.

Palak paneer paratha | Spinach and paneer paratha

MAKES 8

ghee, for cooking
Chilli Chutney (see page 173), to serve

FOR THE DOUGH
200g (7oz) spinach leaves
2 garlic cloves, peeled and roughly chopped
50ml (2fl oz) boiling water
300g (10½oz) chapatti flour, plus extra for dusting
½ teaspoon salt
50ml (2fl oz) cold water

FOR THE FILLING
225g (8oz) paneer, grated
1 red onion, finely chopped
1 green chilli, finely chopped
a handful of fresh coriander, finely chopped
½ teaspoon salt
½ teaspoon chaat masala
½ teaspoon ground cumin

To make the dough, put the spinach and garlic into a large pan, add the boiling water and cook for 5 minutes. Remove from the heat, transfer to a food processor and blitz to a purée.

Put the flour and salt in a large bowl and mix well. Add the spinach purée and mix, slowly adding the cold water to make a soft dough. You might not need all the water or you may need a bit more.

Put all the filling ingredients in a separate bowl and mix well, then divide into 8 equal portions.

Divide the dough into 8 equal portions. Roll out each portion on a flour-dusted work surface to a small disc, about 5–7.5cm (2–3 inches) in diameter. Place a portion of the filling on each disc of dough, then pinch the sides in to cover the filling and seal it in. Press well, then roll each filled parcel of dough out to a small disc, about 10–13cm (4–5 inches) in diameter.

Heat a dry skillet or flat frying pan over a medium heat. Cook each paratha on both sides for 1–2 minutes until they start to turn golden, then add 1 teaspoon of ghee to each side and continue to cook until golden, turning as needed.

Serve immediately with some Chilli Chutney.

Dal pakwaan is a famous Sindhi dish that is made for breakfast. This recipe was kindly given to me by Bhumika, who cooked this delicious lunch for me. A creamy Chana Dal is cooked with just a handful of spices and served with these crispy *pakwaan*. The *pakwaan* can be made beforehand to save you time and will last for 2–3 days in an airtight container. Place a *pakwaan* on a serving plate, top with some dal, Coriander and Ginger Chutney, Tamarind Chutney, chopped onions and fresh coriander, and serve immediately.

Pakwaan | Crispy pastries

MAKES 16

250g (9oz) plain flour
50g (1¾oz) fine semolina
½ teaspoon salt
1 teaspoon cumin seeds
2 tablespoons peanut oil
125ml (4fl oz) water
sunflower oil, for deep-frying

TO SERVE

Chana dal (see page 90)
Coriander and Ginger Chutney (see page 172) or Tamarind Chutney (see page 179)
chopped red onions
fresh coriander (optional)

Combine the flour, semolina, salt, cumin seeds and peanut oil in a bowl and slowly add the water until you have a soft dough. Knead this for 2 minutes, then cover and leave to rest for 30 minutes.

Divide the rested dough into 16 equal portions. Roll out each portion roughly into a thin disc, about 15cm (6 inches) in diameter. Prick each one all over with a fork so that they don't puff up while frying.

Heat enough oil for deep-frying in a large, deep pan to about 170°C (340°F), or until a cube of bread browns in 25 seconds when dropped into the oil. When the oil is hot enough, gently lower each *pakwaan* into the oil one at a time and cook for a minute or so on each side until crispy and golden. Remove with a slotted spoon to drain on kitchen paper.

Serve with Chana dal, your choice of chutney, chopped red onions and fresh coriander, if liked.

Puris carry a lot of meaning for me. When I was growing up, they were made on special occasions – festivals, weddings and picnics – but they are perfect for train journeys, too! I have continued the tradition in my home life today, as I only make *puris* for special days, even if that is just a lovely Sunday afternoon when we can sit together around the table as a family. These spicy *puris* take the humble *puri* and make it the king of the table. A must-try!

Masaledar puri | Spiced-up puri

MAKES 16

1 teaspoon fennel seeds
1 teaspoon coriander seeds
1 teaspoon cumin seeds
1 teaspoon carom seeds
1 teaspoon chilli flakes
½ teaspoon salt
¼ teaspoon asafoetida
1 teaspoon ground turmeric
1 teaspoon chilli powder
200g (7oz) chapatti flour, plus extra for dusting
50g (1¾oz) rice flour
175ml (6fl oz) water
sunflower oil, for deep-frying

Put the fennel, coriander, cumin and carom seeds in a pestle and mortar along with the chilli flakes and crush coarsely. Now add the salt and other spices to the mixture and mix well.

In a large bowl, mix the spices into the flours, then add a little water at a time until you have a soft dough. Divide the dough into 16 equal portions. Roll each one out on a flour-dusted work surface to a thin disc, roughly 7.5–10cm (3–4 inches) in diameter.

Heat enough oil for deep-frying in a large, deep pan to 170°C (340°F) or until a cube of bread browns in 25 seconds when dropped into the oil. When the oil is hot enough, carefully put one *puri* into the hot oil at a time and cook for a minute on each side until golden. Remove with a slotted spoon to drain on kitchen paper.

Serve immediately, either on their own, with pickle or chutney, or any dal or curry of your choice.

I have yet to meet someone who does not like *dosa*. But to make it you have to soak the lentils and rice overnight and then leave the batter to ferment. It is all worth it, but sometimes you want to have it instantly. This recipe will give you a close cousin of *dosa* with all the right crunch and flavour in no time at all. It is best enjoyed with Coconut Sambhar or Onion and Garlic Chutney.

Instant rice dosa

MAKES 8

300g (10½oz) rice flour
1 teaspoon salt
1 teaspoon chilli powder
½ teaspoon ground turmeric
1 teaspoon cumin seeds
1 onion, finely chopped
1 red pepper, finely chopped
1 green chilli, finely chopped
a handful of fresh coriander, finely chopped
400ml (14fl oz) water
100g (3½oz) natural yogurt
sunflower oil, for cooking

TO SERVE
Coconut Sambhar (see page 104), Onion and Garlic Chutney (see page 176) or any other chutney of your choice

Put all the ingredients, except the sunflower oil, in a large bowl and mix well. Cover and leave to stand for 30 minutes.

Heat a frying pan, add a few drops of oil, then wipe with kitchen paper. Now pour one-eighth of the batter mixture into the pan and spread it out evenly. Drizzle a teaspoon of oil all over and cook for 2 minutes, then turn over, drizzle with another teaspoon of oil and cook for 2 more minutes.

Repeat until all the dosas are cooked and then serve with Coconut Sambhar, Onion and Garlic Chutney or any other chutney of your choice.

Sattu is the name for roasted chana dal powder and it is a popular ingredient in many states in India, in particular Bihar. These parathas are nutritious and often eaten as breakfast with a tomato chutney. The roasted chana dal adds such an earthy flavour with a slight crunch from the onion and a great finish with the herbs and lemon. This is an unusual paratha and one you will love. Enjoy it with my Tomato Chutney or some raita.

Sattu paratha | Gram flour-stuffed paratha

MAKES 8

Tomato Chutney (see page 166) or raita, to serve

FOR THE DOUGH

200g (7oz) chapatti flour

100g (3½oz) plain flour, plus extra for dusting

½ teaspoon carom seeds

½ teaspoon nigella seeds

¾ teaspoon salt

200ml (7fl oz) water

ghee, for cooking

FOR THE FILLING

200g (7oz) gram flour (besan)

2.5cm (1 inch) piece of fresh root ginger, peeled and finely chopped

1 onion, finely chopped

4 garlic cloves, finely chopped

1 green chilli, finely chopped

a handful of fresh coriander, finely chopped

2 tablespoons mustard oil

2 tablespoons lemon juice

¾ teaspoon salt

1 teaspoon chilli powder

Put all the dry ingredients for the dough in a bowl and mix well. Slowly add the water to make a soft dough. You might not need all the water or you may need a bit more. Cover and leave to rest for 30 minutes.

Meanwhile, prepare the filling. Dry roast the gram flour over a low heat for 10 minutes until golden and aromatic. This step is really important – keep stirring to ensure that the gram flour is roasted throughout.

Transfer the roasted flour to a bowl and add the rest of the filling ingredients. Rub them together well to obtain a breadcrumb texture.

Divide both the dough and filling into 8 equal portions. Roll out each portion of the dough on a flour-dusted work surface to a rough 10cm (4 inch) disc, then brush with ghee. Place a disc of dough in the palm of your hand, top with one portion of the filling and gather the edges of the dough to seal it in. Press it well, roll it in some more flour, then roll out to a 20cm (8 inch) paratha. Repeat until all are filled and rolled out.

Heat a dry skillet or flat frying pan over a medium heat and cook a paratha on each side for 2 minutes before adding 1 teaspoon of ghee to each side and continuing to cook until crispy and golden. Repeat until all the parathas are cooked.

Serve with some Tomato Chutney or raita.

Bhatura served with *Chole* is a dreamy, classic combination and there is a reason for its popularity – the bhaturas are made with a very light, soft dough which, when fried, puffs up into a ball. Served with creamy chickpeas, they are a delight and an absolute treat. Very popular in the north of India, bhatura are often served at weddings, and are also in demand as street food and great for festivals. Basically, any excuse to make this feast.

Bhatura

MAKES 8

20g (¾oz) fine semolina

about 100ml (3½fl oz) water

300g (10½oz) plain flour, plus extra for dusting

½ teaspoon salt

½ teaspoon sugar

½ teaspoon bicarbonate of soda

4 tablespoons natural yogurt

1 teaspoon sunflower oil, plus extra for deep-frying

Chole (see page 100), to serve

Put the semolina in a small bowl with 50ml (2fl oz) of the water and set aside for 10 minutes.

In another bowl, combine the flour, salt, sugar and bicarbonate of soda, add the soaked semolina and yogurt, then slowly add the remaining water to make a soft dough. You might not need all the water or you may need a bit more. Knead the dough for a minute, then drizzle the teaspoon of oil on top and spread over the surface. Cover and leave to rest for 30 minutes.

Divide the dough into 8 equal portions and shape into balls. Roll out each portion on a flour-dusted work surface to a disc, about 15–18cm (6–7 inches) in diameter.

Heat enough oil for deep-frying in a large, deep pan to 170°C (340°F) or until a cube of bread browns in 25 seconds when dropped into the oil. When the oil is hot enough, place one disc into the oil at a time and let it puff up. Cook for a minute, then turn over and cook for another minute. Remove with a slotted spoon to drain on kitchen paper.

Enjoy immediately with *Chole*.

Bhakri is a staple in many Gujarati kitchens. As Punjabis, chapatti or paratha are things we live on; in just the same way bhakri is an essential part of the meal in Gujarati kitchens. Watching Avani and Renuka prepare these bhakris with such ease and speed in their own kitchens made me smile. These are prepared and served hot, but they are also breads that are made in abundance for travel, and leftovers are enjoyed for breakfast. Whether you have these with just some chutney or a whole feast, it will bring you the same joy and satisfaction.

Bhakri

MAKES 10

300g (10½oz) chapatti flour

½ teaspoon salt

3 tablespoons peanut oil or melted ghee, plus extra ghee for brushing

150ml (5fl oz) water

Put the flour, salt and oil or ghee in a bowl and rub it all together. Slowly add the water to make a slightly stiff dough. This dough is a bit harder than regular chapatti dough, which gives bhakri its characteristic texture. Cover and leave to rest for 10 minutes.

Divide the dough into 10 equal portions, then roll each portion into a small disc roughly 7.5cm (3 inches) in diameter. These are thicker than regular chapatti, so don't be tempted to roll them further.

Heat a dry skillet or flat frying pan over a medium–low heat. Cook each bhakri for 2 minutes on each side until golden. You can even finish cooking them directly on the flame of the hob, turning them with tongs, if you are confident enough.

Once they are cooked, bluntly prick the surface of the bhakri all over with a spoon, brush some ghee on top and serve immediately.

sunflower oil, for
deep-frying

Tari Wale Alu (see page 71),
to serve

FOR THE DOUGH

225g (8oz) chapatti flour,
plus extra for dusting

70g (2½oz) fine semolina

½ teaspoon salt

½ teaspoon carom seeds

1 tablespoon dried fenugreek
leaves (kasuri methi)

1 tablespoon sunflower oil

about 175ml (6fl oz) water

FOR THE FILLING

200g (7oz) urad dal
(white lentils)

400ml (14fl oz) boiling water

4 tablespoons sunflower oil

1 teaspoon cumin seeds

1 teaspoon fennel seeds

¼ teaspoon asafoetida

2.5cm (1 inch) piece of
fresh root ginger, peeled
and finely chopped

1 green chilli, finely chopped

½ teaspoon ground turmeric

1 teaspoon chilli powder

1 teaspoon garam masala

1 teaspoon mango powder
(amchur)

½ teaspoon salt

This *puri* is very popular in the north of India, and mostly served with a delicious *Tari Wale Alu* (potato curry). It's also a street food, famous for being a delicious wholesome breakfast. A few years ago, I remember going to the centre of Old Delhi market early one morning while most of the city was still waking up and there was a queue at the street food stall selling this feast. What a great way to start your day, although I don't think I have ever made this for my breakfast – always a lazy weekend lunch.

Bedmi puri | Dal-stuffed puri

Put all the ingredients for the dough into a bowl, slowly adding the water to form a soft dough. You might not need all the water or you may need more. Knead for a minute, then cover and leave to rest for 1 hour.

Soak the dal for the filling in the boiling water for 1 hour, then drain and blitz to a coarse paste in a food processor with 1–2 tablespoons of water (but make sure it doesn't become runny as you need a thick paste for these). Set aside.

Heat the 4 tablespoons of sunflower oil in a medium pan over a low heat and add the cumin and fennel seeds along with the asafoetida. Once it all starts to sizzle, add the ginger and chilli, and cook for a minute, then add the spices and salt, and mix well. Add the lentil paste and cook over a high heat for 2 minutes. Leave to cool.

Divide both the dough and filling mixtures into 12 equal portions. Roll out each dough portion on a flour-dusted work surface to a 5–7.5cm (2–3 inch) disc. Put a portion of the filling onto each disc of dough and seal in the filling by pinching from all sides. Press each dough ball and roll out to a 10–13cm (4–5 inch) disc.

Heat enough oil for deep-frying in a large, deep pan to 170°C (340°F) or until a cube of bread browns in 25 seconds when dropped into the oil. When the oil is hot enough, deep-fry each *puri*, one at a time, for 2 minutes on each side. Remove with a slotted spoon to drain on kitchen paper.

Serve hot as an accompaniment for *Tari Wale Alu*.

Thepla is a staple in Guajarati kitchens – these flatbreads are made all the time, whether for meals, travel, a picnic or a snack. The dough is spiced up so beautifully and the fresh fenugreek adds a great flavour that binds it all together. Just like everything else, all families have their own *thepla* recipe that is unique to them. This recipe was shared with me by Shimul, who has a love for cooking. Even though she runs a successful travel business, she manages to find time to cook her family's old recipes.

Thepla | Fenugreek flatbreads

MAKES 12

100g (3½oz) fresh fenugreek

300g (10½oz) chapatti flour, plus extra for dusting

2 teaspoons sesame seeds

2 teaspoons jaggery, grated

2.5cm (1 inch) piece of fresh root ginger, peeled and grated

2 teaspoons lemon juice

2 teaspoons peanut oil, plus extra for cooking

1 teaspoon salt

2 green chillies, finely chopped

200ml (7fl oz) water

Pluck the fresh fenugreek leaves off their stems, chop them roughly and place them in a bowl with the rest of the ingredients, except the water. Now add the water slowly to bring it together into a soft dough. Knead for a minute, then cover and leave to rest for 10 minutes.

Divide the dough into 12 equal portions and roll each portion out on a flour-dusted work surface into a thin disc, about 13–15cm (5–6 inches) in diameter.

Heat a dry skillet or flat frying pan over a medium heat. Cook each *thepla*, one at a time, for a minute on each side, then add 1 teaspoon of peanut oil to both sides and cook, turning as needed, until golden.

Taught to me by Meena Aunty, this flatbread is rustic in nature. It is wholesome, packed with nutrition and made in many Gujarati households as part of their staple diet. Characteristically much thicker than normal chapatti, it is cooked slowly over a low heat, then (sometimes) covered in ghee, and is something that people would make for travel food. Leftovers are turned into a sweet with some sugar and ghee. Eaten on its own or with a chutney or curry, this is absolutely delicious.

Rotla

MAKES 4

150g (5½oz) bajra (pearl millet) flour

50g (1¾oz) chapatti flour, plus extra for dusting

½ teaspoon salt

½ teaspoon chilli powder

1 green chilli, finely chopped

a handful of fresh coriander leaves, finely chopped

2 garlic cloves, finely chopped

2 spring onions, finely chopped

150ml (5fl oz) water

melted ghee, to serve

Mix all the ingredients in a large bowl and slowly add the water. You might not need all the water or you may need a bit more. Bring the mixture together into a soft dough and knead for a few seconds. Cover and leave to rest for 15 minutes.

Divide the dough into 4 equal portions. Roll each one in some flour and press out each piece of dough with your hands to a disc about 15–18cm (6–7 inches) in diameter.

Heat a dry skillet or flat frying pan over a low–medium heat. Once this is hot, cook the rotla for 2–3 minutes on each side until they are golden and cooked though. Brush some ghee on top and serve.

RICE

Masala rice 142

Veg tawa pulao 144

Hara adrak pulao | Green ginger pulao 145

Sabzi chole biryani | Vegetable and chickpea biryani 148

Dahi chawal | Yogurt rice 153

Palak ki khichdi | Spinach rice 154

Kadambam | Dal rice 155

Vagharela bhaat | Onion rice 158

Masala Raita (see page 168), to serve

FOR THE MASALA

2 tablespoons coriander seeds

1 star anise

4 green cardamom pods

1 black cardamom pod

2 bay leaves

8 black peppercorns

4 cloves

2 dried red chillies

1 tablespoon sesame seeds

50g (1¾oz) fresh coconut, grated

FOR THE RICE

3 tablespoons sunflower oil

¼ teaspoon asafoetida

1 teaspoon cumin seeds

1 onion, roughly chopped

2.5cm (1 inch) piece of fresh root ginger, peeled and finely chopped

½ cauliflower, cut into florets

1 potato, cut into 2.5cm (1 inch) pieces

125g (4½oz) frozen peas

1 teaspoon salt

½ teaspoon ground turmeric

300g (10½oz) basmati rice

1 tablespoon ghee

700ml (1¼ pints) boiling water

Inspired by the traditional Maharashtrian dish *masale bhat*, this recipe comes from my kitchen. There are many ways of making this rice dish and people use different combinations of vegetables. A staple in many homes, it uses a spice mix called *goda masala*, which is essential. I am using vegetables that grow locally to me and have made a spice mix that is inspired by *goda masala* but is in no way the same, as I am only using a handful of spices whereas many more are used to make the original mix. Enjoy this with some Masala Raita.

Masala rice

For the masala, put all the spices in a large dry pan and roast over a low heat for 2 minutes until aromatic. Now add the sesame seeds and coconut, and cook for a further 2 minutes. Blitz to a powder in a spice grinder.

In the same pan, heat the oil for the rice over a medium heat, add the asafoetida and cumin seeds, let sizzle for a few seconds, then add the onion and cook for 6–8 minutes until golden. Add the ginger and cook for another minute, then add the cauliflower and potato, and cook for 5 minutes.

Add the peas, salt, turmeric and masala followed by the rice and ghee. Mix well. Pour in the boiling water, cover and cook for 15 minutes.

Let the rice sit off the heat for 10 minutes before opening the lid. Serve with Masala Raita.

A popular Mumbai dish, this is very commonly found as street food and also cooked in many ways in different home kitchens. I love this pulao because it has so much going on – with the vegetables, the very sharp chilli garlic paste, and the fluffy rice that brings it all together. A must-try with some Beetroot Raita.

Veg tawa pulao

SERVES 4

4 dried red chillies

8 garlic cloves, peeled

100ml (3½fl oz) boiling water

2 tablespoons salted butter

2 tablespoons sunflower oil

1 teaspoon cumin seeds

1 onion, thinly sliced

1 green pepper, thinly sliced

1 tomato, thinly sliced

1 medium potato, boiled and cut into 2.5cm (1 inch) cubes

1 medium beetroot, grated

½ teaspoon salt

1 teaspoon ground coriander

1 teaspoon garam masala

1 teaspoon mango powder (amchur)

1 teaspoon dried fenugreek leaves (kasuri methi)

20g (¾oz) fresh coriander, finely chopped

600g (1lb 5oz) cooked basmati rice

Beetroot Raita (see page 181), to serve

Soak the dried chillies and garlic cloves in the boiling water for 10 minutes, then blitz it all to a paste (soaking water included) in a food processor. Meanwhile, start cooking the veg.

Heat the butter and oil in a large pan over a medium heat and add the cumin seeds. Once they start to sizzle, add the onion and cook for 5 minutes until starting to soften. Now add the rest of the vegetables and cook over a high heat for 5 minutes more, stirring occasionally.

Add the chilli and garlic paste along with the salt and the rest of the spices, and 100ml (3½fl oz) water. Cook for 5 minutes over a medium heat. Finally, add the coriander and the cooked rice and mix it all well.

Serve with some Beetroot Raita.

This is a stunning pulao using up some seasonal veg and in turn adding all those flavours to the rice. The best bit is that it takes no time to cook at all. You can use other vegetables of your choice, but I have kept them all green and light. This is great served with some raita on the side.

Hara adrak pulao | Green ginger pulao

SERVES 4

4 tablespoons ghee

½ teaspoon asafoetida

1 teaspoon mustard seeds

5cm (2 inch) piece of fresh root ginger, peeled and julienned

10 curry leaves

10 spring onions, chopped

150g (5½oz) sugar snap peas, chopped

10–12 asparagus stems, chopped

1 teaspoon salt

1 teaspoon chilli powder

½ teaspoon ground turmeric

250g (9oz) basmati rice

500ml (18fl oz) boiling water

Heat the ghee in a large pan over a low heat and add the asafoetida. Once it starts to sizzle, add the mustard seeds. Once they start to pop, add the ginger and curry leaves and cook for 1 minute. Add the spring onions, sugar snap peas and asparagus, increase the heat to medium–high and cook for 5 minutes. Now add the salt, chilli powder and turmeric, and mix well.

Add the rice and mix it all well before adding the boiling water. Cover and cook for 15 minutes over a low heat. Turn off the heat and let it rest for 10 minutes before serving.

This is a dish I came up with to entertain the vegetarians in my life, mainly my husband! I love a chicken biryani, it's my death row meal, so I wanted to create a vegetable biryani that could stand side by side with it. I'm pleased to tell you that this one is a winner. You won't miss any meat or flavour in this beautiful layered rice dish. Although biryani was never a vegetarian affair, I am sure it will become a classic in time.

Sabzi chole biryani | Vegetable and chickpea biryani

SERVES 4–6

200ml (7fl oz) sunflower oil

4 onions, thinly sliced

a pinch of saffron

50ml (2fl oz) whole milk, warmed

1 teaspoon rose water

FOR THE VEG

2 bay leaves

6 black peppercorns

6 cloves

1 star anise

1 cinnamon stick

4 cardamom pods

1 teaspoon cumin seeds

2 dried red chillies

2 onions, roughly chopped

2.5cm (1 inch) fresh root ginger, peeled and chopped

4 garlic cloves, finely chopped

2 tomatoes, roughly chopped

1 teaspoon salt

1 teaspoon chilli powder

1 teaspoon ground turmeric

1 teaspoon garam masala

1 teaspoon ground cumin

2 teaspoons ground coriander

½ teaspoon mango powder (amchur)

½ teaspoon black salt (kala namak)

2 carrots, cut into 2.5cm (1 inch) pieces

½ cauliflower, cut into florets

Heat the oil in a large pan over a medium–low heat and cook the onions for 12–15 minutes until golden. Pour into a sieve set over a bowl to collect all the oil. Set the fried onions aside.

Soak the saffron in the warm milk for 10 minutes.

To cook the veg, heat the collected oil in the same pan, add the whole spices and cook for a minute, then add the dried chillies followed by the onions. Cook for 6–8 minutes until golden, then add the ginger and garlic, and cook for another minute. Add the tomatoes and cook for 10 minutes until completely softened.

Now add the salt and all the ground spices and cook for a minute before adding all the veg along with the boiling water. Cook for 5 minutes, then add the yogurt and stir over a very low heat. Cover and cook for 10 minutes until the veg is almost cooked, then add the chickpeas and mix well.

2 potatoes, cut into 2.5cm (1 inch) pieces

150g (5½oz) green beans, cut into 2.5cm (1 inch) pieces

100ml (3½fl oz) boiling water

150g (5½oz) natural yogurt

400g (14oz) tin of chickpeas, drained and rinsed

FOR THE RICE

4 cardamom pods

6 black peppercorns

6 cloves

2 bay leaves

350g (12oz) basmati rice

TO SERVE

raita

Mirchi Ka Salan (see page 79)

For the rice, fill a large pan with water, add the whole spices to it, then add the rice and cook until it is three-quarters cooked. Drain well.

Take a deep stock pan and start layering up the biryani. Put in half of the veg, followed by half of the rice, then half of the fried onions. Repeat with a second layer of each. Drizzle over the rose water and saffron milk. Cover and cook over the lowest heat for 30 minutes. Alternatively, bake in the oven for 30 minutes at 180°C (350°F), Gas Mark 4.

Serve with a raita and *Mirchi Ka Salan*.

This a dish that originated in the south of India. It's called *thayir sadam*, meaning 'curd rice' and another name for it is *daddojanam*. As well as being a staple meal, it is also offered as *prasadam* to devotees in temples. With its many health benefits, it is a cooling light meal, but try it with the Onion and Garlic Chutney (see page 176) or the Coconut Sambhar (see page 104) for an explosion of flavours.

Dahi chawal | Yogurt rice

SERVES 4

500g (1lb 2oz) cooked basmati rice

300g (10½oz) natural yogurt

½ teaspoon salt

FOR THE TADKA

2 teaspoons peanut oil

¼ teaspoon asafoetida

½ teaspoon mustard seeds

½ teaspoon cumin seeds

1 teaspoon chana dal (split yellow peas)

1 teaspoon urad dal (white lentils)

2 dried red chillies

10 curry leaves

2.5cm (1 inch) piece of fresh root ginger, peeled and finely chopped

2 green chillies, slit

8 roasted cashew nuts, roughly chopped

Mash the cooked rice with a fork, add the yogurt and salt to it and mix well.

Heat the oil for the tadka in a pan and add the asafoetida. Once it starts to sizzle, add the mustard and cumin seeds and let sizzle. Reduce the heat, add the chana dal and urad dal and cook for 2 minutes before adding the dried red chillies and curry leaves. After a minute, add the ginger, chillies and cashew nuts, and cook for 2 minutes.

Pour the tadka over the yogurt rice and serve.

Khichdi is one of the most comforting dishes to make when you are hungry, unwell or just need a hug in a bowl. This one is something I created so that I could add more nutrition and some lovely colour to the humble rice dish. Enjoy it with a scoop of yogurt on top or some pickle.

Palak ki khichdi | Spinach rice

SERVES 4

200g (7oz) basmati rice

70g (2½oz) moong dal (split mung beans)

1 teaspoon salt

1 teaspoon ground turmeric

800ml (scant 1½ pints) water

FOR THE SPINACH

250g (9oz) spinach leaves

100ml (3½fl oz) water

FOR THE TADKA

4 tablespoons ghee

1 teaspoon cumin seeds

4 garlic cloves, thinly sliced

Put the rice, moong dal, salt, turmeric and water in a saucepan and bring to the boil. Cover and cook for 20 minutes over a low heat until the rice and dal are cooked, soft and broken up.

Put the spinach into a separate pan along with the water, cover and cook for 5 minutes until wilted. Use a hand-held blender to blitz it to a purée, then add it to the dal and rice mix. If the mixture is too thick, add another 100ml (3½fl oz) of boiling water.

Heat the ghee for the tadka in a small pan and add the cumin seeds. Once they start to sizzle, add the garlic and cook for 1 minute until it starts to change colour. Pour this over the cooked *khichdi* and serve.

Kadambam means a combination of different things that come together. This is a recipe that is traditionally cooked in temples as *prasadam* (an offering to a god) during the *Dusshera* festival, so it does not contain onions or garlic. People add different veg to this dish – my selection of veg in this recipe is small and I have used things that should be easily available. I am also finishing this dish with a tadka, which is not a common practice.

Kadambam | Dal rice

SERVES 4

FOR THE RICE

250g (9oz) basmati rice

125g (4½oz) toor dal (split pigeon peas)

125g (4½oz) moong dal (split mung beans)

1.2 litres (2 pints) water

1 teaspoon salt

1 teaspoon ground turmeric

FOR THE VEG

1 potato, cut into 2.5cm (1 inch) chunks

1 aubergine, cut into 2.5cm (1 inch) chunks

2 drumsticks (moringa pods), strings removed, cut into 4cm (1½ inch) pieces

10 curry leaves

1 teaspoon salt

1 teaspoon ground turmeric

FOR THE TAMARIND WATER

50g (1¾oz) tamarind pulp

100ml (3½fl oz) boiling water

FOR THE TADKA

4 tablespoons ghee

2 dried red chillies

10 curry leaves

Put the rice and dals in a pan along with the water and leave to soak for 1 hour.

Add the salt and turmeric to the rice/dal pan and bring to the boil, then reduce to a simmer and cook for 30 minutes until everything is cooked through and soft.

In a separate large pan, combine the veg, curry leaves, salt and turmeric with 200ml (7fl oz) water. Bring to the boil, cover and cook for 5 minutes.

To make the tamarind water, put the tamarind pulp in a bowl, cover with the boiling water and leave to soak for 5 minutes. Strain the tamarind water through a sieve into a small bowl, squeezing the pulp to extract as much flavour as possible.

Add the tamarind water to the veg along with the rice and lentil mix, and combine it all well.

Prepare the tadka by heating the ghee in a small pan, then add the chillies and curry leaves.

Immediately pour the tadka over the prepared dish and serve.

Bhaat means 'rice' and this is a delicious way to use up leftover rice. It is an old recipe and people have their own way of preparing it. Some add more vegetables, some add buttermilk, but this is the most common Gujarati way to make it. To be honest, I would happily make fresh rice just to make this recipe, it's so good!

Vagharela bhaat | Onion rice

SERVES 4

4 tablespoons peanut oil

1 teaspoon mustard seeds

¼ teaspoon asafoetida

10 curry leaves

2 green chillies, thinly sliced

2 medium onions, finely chopped

1 teaspoon salt

1 teaspoon chilli powder

1 teaspoon ground turmeric

1 teaspoon ground cumin

500g (1lb 2oz) cooked basmati rice

Heat the oil in a large pan over a medium heat, add the mustard seeds and asafoetida. Once they start to sizzle, add the curry leaves and chillies, cook for a few seconds, then add the onions and cook for 5 minutes until softened. Add the salt and the spices and mix well, then add the rice and mix well. Cook over a high heat for 3–4 minutes until heated through. Serve.

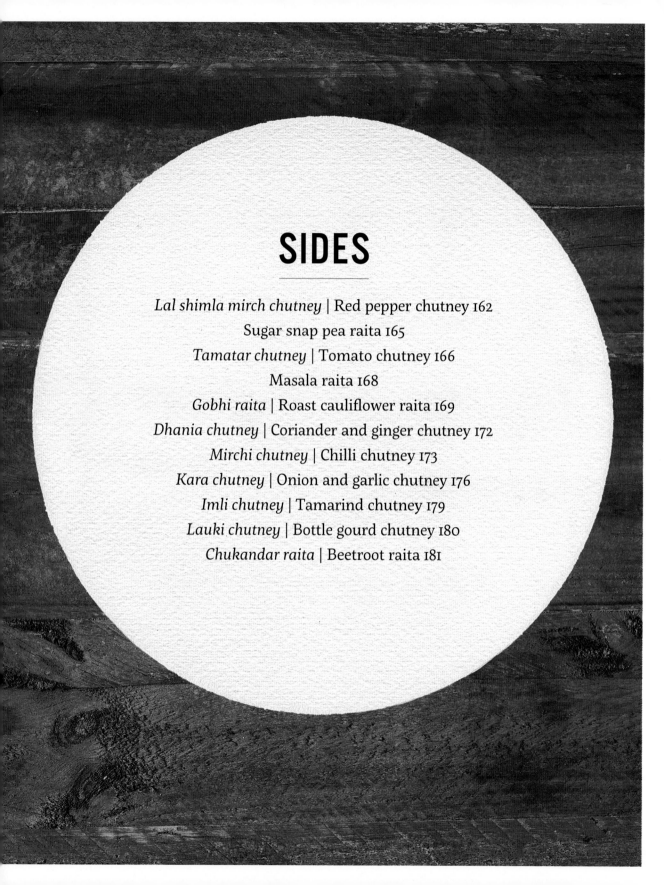

SIDES

Lal shimla mirch chutney | Red pepper chutney 162

Sugar snap pea raita 165

Tamatar chutney | Tomato chutney 166

Masala raita 168

Gobhi raita | Roast cauliflower raita 169

Dhania chutney | Coriander and ginger chutney 172

Mirchi chutney | Chilli chutney 173

Kara chutney | Onion and garlic chutney 176

Imli chutney | Tamarind chutney 179

Lauki chutney | Bottle gourd chutney 180

Chukandar raita | Beetroot raita 181

Red peppers cooked with a handful of crunchy, creamy and spicy ingredients makes for a delicious chutney, and the tadka drizzled on top adds to the flavour and finish.

Lal shimla mirch chutney | Red pepper chutney

MAKES A SMALL BOWL

2 tablespoons peanut oil

2 teaspoons chana dal (split yellow peas)

2 teaspoons urad dal (white lentils)

2 teaspoons sesame seeds

30g (1oz) unsalted raw peanuts (with skins)

¼ teaspoon asafoetida

2 dried red chillies

2 red peppers, roughly chopped

50g (1¾oz) fresh coconut, grated or finely chopped

100ml (3½fl oz) water

juice of ½ lemon

FOR THE TADKA

2 tablespoons peanut oil

1 teaspoon mustard seeds

2 dried red chillies

Heat the oil in a pan, add the dals and cook over a low heat for 2 minutes. Add the sesame seeds and peanuts, cook for another minute, then add the asafoetida. Next, add the dried red chillies and cook for a minute, then add the red peppers and cook over a low–medium heat for 15 minutes.

Add the coconut, water and lemon juice, and cook for a further 10 minutes until most of the water has cooked out. Let cool for a few minutes before blitzing to a paste in a food processor.

Heat the oil for the tadka in a small pan, add the mustard seeds and dried chillies and let sizzle for a few seconds before pouring over the chutney.

Store in an airtight container in the refrigerator for 3–4 days.

When Shimul mentioned a radish pod raita to me, I got really excited and it did not disappoint. But then I started to think about the ease of actually finding radish pods, a seasonal vegetable in India, elsewhere and it got me thinking. I decided to give Shimul's raita a go using sugar snap peas instead. Although it tasted different, it had great texture and flavour – a perfect raita. So here you have a choice: make it with sugar snaps or radish pods, whatever you can get your hands on.

Sugar snap pea raita

SERVES 4

3 tablespoons ghee

1 teaspoon mustard seeds

¼ teaspoon asafoetida

2 teaspoons urad dal (white lentils)

2.5cm (1 inch) piece of fresh root ginger, peeled and grated

200g (7oz) sugar snap peas, thinly sliced

1 red chilli, thinly sliced

250g (9oz) natural yogurt

¼ teaspoon salt

½ teaspoon chilli powder

50ml (2fl oz) water

a pinch of red chilli flakes

Heat the ghee in a medium pan, add the mustard seeds and asafoetida, and let sizzle for a few seconds. Now add the urad dal and cook over a low heat for 2 minutes. Don't let it colour too much. Add the ginger and cook for 1 minute, then add the sugar snap peas and red chilli. Slowly cook for 10 minutes until they have softened, then remove from the heat and leave to cool.

In a bowl, mix the yogurt with the salt, chilli powder and water, and whisk until smooth. Add the cooked sugar snaps and mix well, then sprinkle with the red chilli flakes and serve.

Chutneys are flavour bombs – add a tablespoon here and there and your meal changes completely, always for the better. Whether having it with snacks or as a side to a meal, this tomato chutney is spicy, creamy because of the aubergine, and with a tomatoey tang – a winner!

Tamatar chutney | Tomato chutney

MAKES A SMALL BOWL

4 tomatoes, roughly chopped

2 green chillies, roughly chopped

4 garlic cloves, roughly chopped

1 aubergine

4 tablespoons peanut oil, plus extra for brushing

¼ teaspoon asafoetida

½ teaspoon salt

½ teaspoon chilli powder

½ teaspoon ground turmeric

a handful of fresh coriander, chopped

In a food processor, blitz the tomatoes, chillies and garlic to a paste.

Preheat the grill to high.

Prick the aubergine all over with a knife and brush with a little oil. Roast under the hot grill for 15 minutes, turning occasionally, until the skin is blackened and blistered.

Meanwhile, heat the oil in a pan, add the asafoetida and let it sizzle. Add the tomato paste and cook over a medium heat for 10 minutes until it goes a bit deeper in colour, reduces and gets thicker.

Let the aubergine cool slightly, then halve it and scrape out the soft insides. Add to the pan with the tomatoes along with the salt and spices, and cook for a final 5 minutes.

Remove from the heat, add the chopped coriander and mix well. You can serve this chutney warm or at room temperature.

Raita is the perfect cooling accompaniment to an Indian meal. This one has all the ingredients of a great masala; when added to yogurt, it really brings it to life.

Masala raita

SERVES 4

2 tablespoons sunflower oil

1 onion, finely chopped

1 green chilli, finely chopped

2.5cm (1 inch) piece of fresh root ginger, peeled and finely chopped

1 tomato, finely chopped

½ teaspoon chilli powder

½ teaspoon ground turmeric

½ teaspoon salt

300g (10½oz) natural yogurt

FOR THE TADKA

2 tablespoons sunflower oil

1 teaspoon mustard seeds

1 teaspoon urad dal (white lentils)

a handful of fresh coriander leaves, finely chopped

Heat the oil in a pan over a medium heat, add the onion and chilli, and cook for 5 minutes until softened. Add the ginger and cook for a minute, then add the tomato and cook for 5 minutes until softened. Add the spices and salt, and remove from the heat to cool slightly.

Once it has cooled, add the masala to the yogurt and mix together well.

Heat the oil for the tadka in a small pan, add the mustard seeds and urad dal and cook over a low heat for 2 minutes. Add the coriander and mix well, then pour over the yogurt and serve.

I am a big fan of cauliflower – it's something that comes across in my recipes, as I love to cook it in different ways. Here, I have roasted it with a few lovely spices and served it with a lightly spiced yogurt, making it the perfect side dish for a meal.

Gobhi raita | Roast cauliflower raita

SERVES 4

3 tablespoons chilli oil or sunflower oil

70g (2½oz) tomato purée

1 teaspoon salt

2 teaspoons curry powder

1 medium cauliflower, cut into florets

a few mint leaves, roughly torn

FOR THE YOGURT

300g (10½oz) natural yogurt

50ml (2fl oz) water

a pinch of salt

a pinch of black pepper

¼ teaspoon ground cumin

Preheat the oven to 200°C (400°F), Gas Mark 6.

In a small bowl, mix together the oil, tomato purée, salt and curry powder. Place the cauliflower florets on a baking tray, put the paste on top and mix it all well. Roast in the oven for 15 minutes, then turn the cauliflower florets over and return to the oven to roast for another 15 minutes.

In a medium bowl, mix the yogurt with the water, salt and spices and spread it over a serving plate. Place the roasted cauliflower florets on top, sprinkle with the mint and serve.

As always, here is a new and delicious version of my favourite chutney ever – coriander chutney. In this recipe I have added some ginger and cumin with black salt to give it a slightly different flavour. Enjoy with absolutely everything you decide to cook from this book.

Dhania chutney | Coriander and ginger chutney

MAKES A SMALL BOWL

85g (3oz) fresh coriander, leaves and stalks

10g (¼oz) mint leaves

1cm (½ inch) piece of fresh root ginger, peeled

2 green chillies

½ teaspoon caster sugar

¼ teaspoon salt

¼ teaspoon black salt (kala namak)

½ teaspoon ground cumin

juice of ½ lemon

ice cubes

Put all the chutney ingredients in a blender with 1 or 2 ice cubes and blitz to a paste. Serve fresh.

Hot, hot, hot – be careful with this one! I love that this chutney is spicy, like the name suggests, but that should not stop you from eating it. The heat is intense, but the flavour is strong too. It also keeps well, so even more reason to make some.

Mirchi chutney | Chilli chutney

MAKES A SMALL BOWL

20 dried Kashmiri chillies

2 tablespoons water

10 garlic cloves, roughly chopped

1 tomato, roughly chopped

4 tablespoons peanut oil

1 teaspoon mustard seeds

¼ teaspoon asafoetida

1 tablespoon urad dal (white lentils)

3 tablespoons jaggery, grated

1 tablespoon tamarind paste

1 teaspoon salt

Soak the chillies in boiling water for 15 minutes, then transfer the chillies to a blender along with the water, the garlic and tomato, and blitz to a purée.

Heat the oil in a pan and add the mustard seeds and asafoetida. Once they start to pop, add the urad dal and cook over a low heat for 2 minutes. Once the dal starts to change colour, add the chilli purée and continue to cook over a low heat for 15 minutes.

Now add the jaggery, tamarind and salt, and cook for 2 minutes until the jaggery has dissolved. Let it cool before serving.

You can store this in an airtight jar in the refrigerator for up to 2 weeks.

This chutney is inspired by the very famous *kara chutney* from Tamil Nadu. As with many other recipes, you will find hundreds of variations of this chutney, different in every household. And like many chutneys, this one is packed with flavour and will leave you wanting to have it with every meal.

Kara chutney | Onion and garlic chutney

MAKES A SMALL BOWL

6 tablespoons peanut oil

1 tablespoon chana dal (split yellow peas)

1 teaspoon urad dal (white lentils)

6 dried red chillies

2.5cm (1 inch) piece of fresh root ginger, peeled and roughly chopped

10 garlic cloves, peeled

2 onions, roughly chopped

2 tomatoes, roughly chopped

2 tablespoons water

½ teaspoon salt

FOR THE TADKA

2 tablespoons peanut oil

1 teaspoon mustard seeds

10 curry leaves

Heat the peanut oil in a medium pan over a low heat, add the chana dal and urad dal and cook for 1 minute. Next, add the red chillies, ginger and garlic and cook for another 2 minutes. Add the onions and cook for 3–4 minutes until they start to soften, then add the tomatoes and water, cover and cook for 5 minutes until softened. Add the salt, then transfer the mixture to a food processor and blitz to a purée.

Heat the oil for the tadka in a small pan and add the mustard seeds. Once they start to pop, add the curry leaves then remove from the heat.

Pour the tadka over the chutney and serve, either warm or at room temperature.

Store the chutney in an airtight container in the refrigerator for 3–4 days.

A must if you are making any kind of Indian *chaat* and if you have ever had *chaat* you will know why. It is sour, slightly sweet and utterly refreshing. Don't limit it to the *chaat* though; enjoy it with all sorts of snacks too.

Imli chutney | Tamarind chutney

MAKES A SMALL BOWL

100g (3½oz) tamarind pulp

50g (1¾oz) dates, stones removed, roughly chopped

200ml (7fl oz) water

100g (3½oz) jaggery

½ teaspoon ground ginger

1 teaspoon cumin seeds, roasted and crushed

½ teaspoon chilli powder

Put the tamarind pulp, dates and water in a pan and cook over a low heat for 10 minutes. Add the jaggery and cook for another 10 minutes until everything is soft and cooked through.

Pass the mixture through a sieve into a jug, pressing the pulp to get all the flavour out.

Transfer the mixture in the jug back to the pan, heat it through and add the spices.

When cooled, if you don't use it straight away, you can store it in a sterilized jar in the refrigerator for 3–4 weeks. When using, you might want to add a bit more water to thin it out to your preference.

Also known as *sorakaya pachadi* in Telugu language, this chutney is served with rice and most South Indian dishes. The recipe was given to me by Radhika, my friend who cooks amazing South Indian food – her chutneys are legendary.

Lauki chutney | Bottle gourd chutney

MAKES A SMALL BOWL

1 tablespoon chana dal (split yellow peas)

1 tablespoon urad dal (white lentils)

2 tablespoons unsalted roasted peanuts

1 tablespoon sesame seeds

3 tablespoons peanut oil

1 medium bottle gourd (lauki), about 300g (10½oz), peeled and roughly chopped

1 tomato, roughly chopped

1 green chilli, roughly chopped

¾ teaspoon salt

½ teaspoon sugar

1 teaspoon tamarind paste

FOR THE TADKA

2 tablespoons peanut oil

1 teaspoon urad dal (white lentils)

1 green chilli, finely chopped

Dry roast the dals, peanuts and sesame seeds in a dry pan for 2 minutes until fragrant and lightly golden, then blitz to a powder in a spice grinder.

Heat the oil in a large pan over a medium heat, add the gourd and cook for 5–6 minutes until softened, then add the tomato and green chilli and cook for another 5 minutes. Transfer to a food processor and blitz to a purée, then return the mixture to the pan. Add the blitzed dal powder along with the salt, sugar and tamarind paste, and mix well. Cook for a minute until the sugar has dissolved.

Heat the oil for the tadka in a separate small pan, add the urad dal and, after a minute, add the chilli. Drizzle the tadka over the chutney.

Serve at room temperature and store leftovers in the refrigerator for 3–4 days.

A pretty pink number for your meal, with a tang of sweet and earthy flavours beautifully combined. You can prepare the raita beforehand and let it chill in the refrigerator until you are ready to serve. Just make and pour the tadka right before serving. This is great with any Indian meal.

Chukandar raita | Beetroot raita

SERVES 4

300ml (10fl oz) natural yogurt

½ teaspoon salt

½ teaspoon sugar

½ teaspoon chilli powder

½ teaspoon ground cumin

1 beetroot, peeled and grated

FOR THE TADKA

2 tablespoons ghee

1 teaspoon mustard seeds

10 curry leaves

Mix all the ingredients for the raita together in a bowl.

When ready to serve, heat the ghee for the tadka in a small pan, add the mustard seeds and curry leaves and let it all sizzle. Pour over the raita and serve.

SWEET

Sukdi | Jaggery treat 186

Balushahi 189

Khaman ghari 190

Ras malai 192

Chiroti 193

Mysore pak 196

Puran poli laddoo 197

Gur chawal ki kheer | Jaggery rice kheer 200

Lapsi 203

Churma 204

Nariyal barfi | Coconut barfi 205

Sukdi is a traditional sweet that has been made in Gujarati kitchens for generations. This stunningly delicious treat is served in temples as *prasaad* (offerings to a god) but is also made at home for a snack and is perfect as travel food, too. When I visited Avani, she made this *sukdi* for me in minutes. It is something she often makes for her family as a pick-me-up. There was a time when ghee and jaggery were considered to give you strength and nourishment – we seem to have forgotten that. Nowadays, we prefer to eat them in small portions and enjoy them as a treat or snack, rather than as a meal.

Sukdi | Jaggery treat

SERVES 16

160g (5¾oz) melted ghee, plus extra for greasing

160g (5¾oz) chapatti flour

160g (5¾oz) jaggery, grated

a handful of pistachios, thinly sliced

Grease a shallow baking tray, roughly 23 × 15cm (9 × 6 inches), with some ghee.

In a frying pan, dry-roast the chapatti flour and ghee over a low heat for 15 minutes until you can smell the aroma and it turns a light caramel colour. Remove the pan from the heat and add the jaggery, stirring continuously until the jaggery has dissolved.

Scrape the mixture into the prepared tray and spread evenly. Sprinkle over the pistachios and press them in gently. Let it cool slightly, then use a knife to mark diamond shapes on it. Leave to cool completely before serving, cut into diamond shapes. These will last in a box for a good week.

Like a lot of Indian sweets, this is a rich sugary delight – a light dough fried and then bathed in sugar syrup. When I was growing up, my *Nanaji* (grandfather) used to bring piping hot balushahi home from the shops in the evenings, whenever we would go to stay for summer holidays. I could never recreate that dessert and have not been back to that town in decades, so I had to go by what my senses and understanding of Indian sweets could produce. Although it's not authentic, this is delicious and is something that I have started making for special occasions.

Balushahi

MAKES 12

50g (1¾oz) softened ghee (not melted)

50g (1¾oz) Greek yogurt

200g (7oz) plain flour

½ teaspoon baking powder

¼ teaspoon bicarbonate of soda

70ml (2½fl oz) water

sunflower oil or ghee, for deep-frying

FOR THE SUGAR SYRUP

200g (7oz) caster sugar

150ml (5fl oz) water

a pinch of saffron

8–10 cardamom pods, bashed

Put the softened ghee in a bowl and whisk for 1 minute until smooth and one shade lighter. Now add the yogurt and mix again.

In a separate bowl, mix the flour, baking powder and bicarbonate of soda together thoroughly, then sift into the ghee bowl and fold in with a spoon. Slowly add the water and bring the mixture together into a soft dough. You might not need all the water or you may need a bit more. Don't knead the dough or the balushahi will harden. This is like shortcrust pastry, so don't handle too much. Cover and leave to rest for 10 minutes.

Meanwhile, prepare the sugar syrup. Heat the sugar and water in a pan until the sugar has dissolved. Now add the saffron and cardamom and stir through. Cook for 2 minutes, then set aside.

Heat the oil or ghee for deep-frying in a large, deep pan to 130°C (270°F) or until a cube of bread browns in 1 minute when dropped into the oil. When the oil is hot enough, add the dough balls, a few at a time. Cook over a low heat for 5 minutes, then increase the heat to 170°C (340°F) and cook for another 8–10 minutes until the balls are a deep golden colour. Remove them with a slotted spoon and drain them on kitchen paper.

Drop the hot balushahi into the sugar syrup and leave for a few minutes to soak. Remove and serve warm.

This is one of the special recipes I learned while in Ahmedabad. When I went to visit Kety Aunty in her Parsi community kitchen, I was welcomed by a lovely group of women who were all smiles and chatting and cooking together. They were preparing food for the community lunch boxes and I was especially interested in these khaman ghari as I'd never had them before. You won't find this recipe on the internet as it is dying out and only known to a remaining few. When they came out of the oven I couldn't stop eating them. I knew that this would be a recipe I would treasure, and I hope you will too.

Khaman ghari

MAKES 4

FOR THE DOUGH

250g (9oz) plain flour, plus extra for dusting

25g (1oz) fine semolina

a pinch of salt

25g (1oz) ghee, melted

140ml (4½fl oz) water

FOR THE FILLING

200g (7oz) fresh coconut, grated or blitzed to a coarse mix

200g (7oz) caster sugar

100g (3½oz) ghee

100ml (3½fl oz) water

1 teaspoon ground cardamom

a sprinkle of fresh grated nutmeg

1 teaspoon vanilla extract

50g (1¾oz) raisins, finely chopped

2 tablespoons ground almonds

FOR THE RICE PASTE

50g (1¾oz) rice flour

50g (1¾oz) ghee, melted

For the dough, put the flour, semolina and salt in a bowl. Add the ghee and rub it into the flour. Now add the water a little at a time to make a soft dough. You might not need all the water or you may need a bit more. Knead for 1 minute, then cover and leave to rest for 30 minutes.

Meanwhile, prepare the filling. Put the coconut, sugar, ghee and water in a pan and mix well. Cook over a low heat for 30 minutes, stirring until the mixture starts to thicken and leave the sides of the pan. Transfer to a bowl and stir for 2 minutes to cool it slightly, then add the rest of the filling ingredients and mix well.

For the rice paste, mix together the rice flour and melted ghee in a bowl and set aside.

Preheat the oven to 220°C (425°F), Gas Mark 7. Line 2 baking trays with baking paper.

Divide the dough into 3 portions. Roll out each portion on a flour-dusted work surface to a disc, about 30cm (12 inches) in diameter. Spread a heaped tablespoon of the rice paste on each of the discs, then pile them on top of one another. Roll the stack up tightly, then cut the roll into 4 equal portions.

Roll out each portion to a disc around 10cm (4 inches) in diameter and fill each disc with roughly one-sixth of the filling, or as much as you can (you may have a little left over). Pinch the sides of the dough in to seal the filling inside, then gently press out to a 15cm (6 inch) disc.

Place the filled breads on the baking trays and bake for 15 minutes until golden and crispy. Serve immediately.

Ras malai is a very popular Indian dessert, often made for weddings and special occasions. It is super simple to make with the fewest of ingredients. Made with *rasgulla*, the spongy little sweets that are sold in almost all Indian sweet shops, and then soaked in thick, sweet milk, it just melts in your mouth. A must-try!

Ras malai

MAKES 14

FOR THE *RASGULLA*
1 litre (1¾ pints) whole milk
juice of 1 lemon
1 tablespoon cornflour

FOR THE SUGAR SYRUP
200g (7oz) granulated sugar
700ml (1¼ pints) water
4 cardamom pods, smashed

FOR THE MILK
1 litre (1¾ pints) whole milk
a pinch of saffron
4 tablespoons condensed milk
4 cardamom pods

TO SERVE
50g (1¾oz) pistachios, finely chopped

For the *rasgulla*, put the milk in a pan and bring it to the boil. Add the lemon juice and mix well, then remove from the heat and set aside for 5 minutes.

Place a muslin cloth over a sieve, then drain the milk mixture through the muslin (this will collect all the milk solids and drain the whey). Gather in the sides of the cloth and twist to get rid of all the excess liquid, then place a couple of tins or a heavy pestle on top of the muslin while it sits in the sieve and leave for 10 minutes.

Next, make the sugar syrup. Put the sugar, water and cardamom pods in a saucepan and bring to the boil. Turn the heat off once the sugar has completely dissolved.

Take the *chenna* (milk solids) from the muslin and place on a clean surface. Sprinkle the cornflour on top and start kneading with the palm of your hand. Continue for 10 minutes until the

mixture comes together into a smooth, soft dough. Divide this into 14 portions and shape into smooth balls.

Return the sugar syrup to the boil, then gently place the *chenna* balls into the hot syrup, cover and cook over a low heat for 15 minutes until the balls have doubled in size and are soft and spongy.

Meanwhile, heat the milk and saffron in a separate pan for 30 minutes over a low heat, stirring occasionally. Add the condensed milk and cardamom, and mix well. Pour into a serving dish.

One by one, remove each *rasgulla* from the sugar syrup and press to remove excess syrup, then dip into the perfumed milk to coat. Leave them in the dish to serve and sprinkle the pistachios on top.

These are great served warm or chilled. They will keep in an airtight container in the refrigerator for 2–3 days.

This crispy layered sweet has many incarnations, made in different shapes and with different names in different parts of India. It is called chiroti in Maharashtra and Karnataka, but in Bihar and Andhra Pradesh it is called *khaja*. I am very sure it has other names, too. It takes a little bit of effort to roll the dough out, but you will thank yourself with every mouthful.

Chiroti

MAKES 30

sunflower oil, for
deep-frying

FOR THE DOUGH

150g (5½oz) fine semolina

150g (5½oz) plain flour,
plus extra for dusting

3 tablespoons ghee

about 125ml (4fl oz) water

FOR THE PASTE

70g (2½oz) unsalted butter,
softened

50g (1¾oz) rice flour

FOR THE SYRUP

200g (7oz) caster sugar

200ml (7fl oz) water

6-8 cardamom pods,
smashed

For the dough, mix the semolina and flour in a bowl. Add the ghee and rub it in well, then slowly add the water to make a soft dough. You might not need all the water or you may need more. Knead for a minute, then cover and leave to rest for 30 minutes.

Meanwhile, prepare the paste, mixing together the butter and rice flour in a small bowl until smooth.

Divide the dough in half and cut each half into 5 equal portions. Roll out the first 5 portions on a flour-dusted work surface to thin discs, each 20–23cm (8–9 inches) in diameter. Evenly spread 1 teaspoon or so of the paste over the first disc, then place another disc on top. Repeat until all 5 layers are stacked up together. Now roll the stack up tightly and cut into 1cm (½ inch) slices. You should be able to get 14–15 slices from this one roll. Repeat with the other half of the dough.

In a small pan, heat the sugar and water with the cardamom pods until the sugar has melted. Let it simmer for 2 minutes, then remove from the heat.

Meanwhile, heat enough oil for deep-frying in a large, deep pan to 150°C (300°F) or until a cube of bread browns in 45 seconds when dropped into the oil. When the oil is hot enough, take each piece of pastry and press it out by hand to a 5cm (2 inch) disc. Carefully lower into the hot oil and cook in batches for 8–10 minutes until deep golden and crispy. Remove each chiroti with a slotted spoon to a plate, then transfer to the sugar syrup, turning them until coated. Remove to another plate.

You can enjoy these warm or at room temperature. They will keep for a couple of days in an airtight container.

This recipe is rumoured to have originated in the royal kitchen of the Mysore maharaja's palace. It is a very popular sweet in the southern states of Karnataka and Tamil Nadu and is made with only three ingredients. The key to this recipe is timing – it is ready swiftly. You just need to get the sugar to the right consistency and then it takes only a few minutes, so you can't take your eye off the ball or stop that stirring.

Mysore pak

SERVES 6–8

200g (7oz) ghee, plus extra for greasing
200g (7oz) caster sugar
150ml (5fl oz) water
100g (3½oz) gram flour (besan), sifted

Grease a 900g (2lb) loaf tin.

Heat the ghee in a pan until melted and warmed through.

Heat the sugar and water in a separate pan (avoid using a nonstick pan for this recipe). Once the sugar has dissolved, continue to cook the syrup until you reach 'one string' consistency, just below 100°C (212°F). (To check this without a thermometer, put a few drops of syrup in a bowl and let cool slightly. Dip a finger in the syrup and rub it between your finger and thumb. When you gently pull your finger and thumb apart, a single firm string should form.)

Add 2 tablespoons of the flour and continue to stir until combined, then add another 2 tablespoons of the flour and stir. Add the remaining flour and continue to stir.

Now add a third of the ghee and stir until combined, then add another third of the ghee and stir until combined. Add the final third of the ghee and stir until combined and the mixture looks as though it is breaking apart.

Immediately pour this into the prepared tin and spread evenly. Leave to set for 15 minutes before removing from the tin and slicing into fingers.

When I asked my cousin Nimisha to cook something sweet for me, she suggested these *laddoos* and I was intrigued. I have enjoyed *puran poli* (a popular Maharashtrian dish of sweet flatbreads) all my life but had never heard of these *laddoos*. Then I found out that these soft lentil balls in a thin, slightly crispy batter are also called *poornam boorelu* in Andhra Pradesh, and are a special treat made for festivals, weddings and special occasions.

Puran poli laddoo

MAKES 20–22

100g (3½oz) basmati rice

50g (1¾oz) urad dal (white lentils)

300g (10½oz) chana dal (split yellow peas)

900ml (generous 1½ pints) water

200g (7oz) jaggery, grated

½ teaspoon ground cardamom

a pinch of freshly grated nutmeg

85g (3oz) fresh coconut, grated

sunflower oil, for deep-frying

Soak the rice and urad dal separately in plenty of water overnight, or for at least 6 hours.

Soak the chana dal in a saucepan with the water for 1 hour, then bring to the boil and cook for 30–35 minutes until the dal is soft and breaks down with hardly any water left. Add the jaggery and mix well, then cook for a further 10 minutes until the jaggery has dissolved and the dal has dried out. Add the cardamom, nutmeg and grated coconut, and mix well. Set aside to cool down.

Drain the rice and blitz it to a fine paste in a food processor or with a stick blender along with 2–3 tablespoons of water. Drain the urad dal and blitz it to a fine paste with 3–4 tablespoons of water.

Now mix both the pastes together and add another 2–3 tablespoons of water to make a thick batter (it should have the consistency of thick pancake batter).

Divide the cooled filling mixture into 20–22 equal portions and shape them into balls.

Heat enough oil for deep-frying in a large, deep pan to 170°C (340°F) or until a cube of bread browns in 25 seconds when dropped into the oil. When the oil is hot enough, dip the balls into the batter in batches until well coated, then lower into the hot oil. Cook for 4–6 minutes, making sure to turn them over as needed, until lightly golden. Remove with a slotted spoon to drain on kitchen paper.

Serve warm or at room temperature.

This is one of my favourite Indian desserts. I can still taste the kheer my mum makes – creamy, soft, delicious and so wholesome. I am making this with jaggery, which adds another layer of deep flavour. The best part is that it can be served warm or cold. Opinion is divided as to what is the better way to enjoy this, so make up your own mind.

Gur chawal ki kheer | Jaggery rice kheer

SERVES 4

100g (3½oz) basmati rice

1.2 litres (2 pints) whole milk

1 teaspoon ground cardamom

70g (2½oz) jaggery, grated

10g (¼oz) pistachios, chopped

10g (¼oz) almonds, chopped

10g (¼oz) raisins, chopped

Soak the rice in water for 30 minutes, then drain and lightly crush in a pestle and mortar until the rice grains break. Don't crush to make a paste, just break the grains up.

In a large pan, bring the milk to the boil and add the crushed rice. Cook over a low heat for 30–35 minutes until the rice is fully cooked. Add the cardamom and jaggery, and cook for a further 5 minutes until the jaggery has dissolved.

Sprinkle the kheer with the chopped nuts and raisins, and serve warm or cold.

Lapsi is a traditional Gujarati sweet dish which is made to mark festivities or special occasions. It is made with *fada* (broken or cracked wheat), lots of ghee and sugar, and cooked in a pressure cooker to speed up the process. It's so rich, sweet and moreish. Here I am using bulgur wheat, as it is easier to find, tastes almost the same and reduces the cooking time.

Lapsi

SERVES 4

20g (¾oz) ghee

100g (3½oz) bulgur wheat

400ml (14fl oz) water

50g (1¾oz) caster sugar

10g (¼oz) raisins, chopped

10g (¼oz) cashew nuts, chopped

½ teaspoon ground cardamom

10g (¼oz) fresh coconut, grated

Put the ghee and bulghur wheat in a pan and cook over a low heat for 5 minutes until the bulgur is fluffy, fragrant, swells up and turns a bit golden. Remove from the heat.

Add the water, then return to the heat and cook for 25 minutes until soft and most of the water has been absorbed. Add the sugar and cook until dissolved.

Add the raisins, cashew nuts, cardamom and grated coconut, and serve.

Dal, bati and churma is a classic combination that is often served together. The savoury Mixed Dal (see page 101) and *Bati* (see page 116) combined with the mild sweetness of the churma make the dish extraordinary. The churma is usually made with the same dough as the *bati* but sometimes extra dough is made just to put the churma together. Of course, this doesn't mean you can't eat churma on its own, as it's a dessert you need to try.

Churma

SERVES 4

FOR THE DOUGH
125g (4½oz) chapatti flour
a pinch of salt
a pinch of bicarbonate of soda
2 tablespoons ghee
50ml (2fl oz) water
sunflower oil, for deep-frying

TO FINISH
4 tablespoons ghee
25g (1oz) icing sugar
1 teaspoon ground cardamom
12 cashew nuts, finely chopped
12 almonds, finely chopped

For the dough, put the flour, salt and bicarbonate of soda in a bowl and add the ghee. Rub the ghee into the flour then slowly add the water to make a soft dough. Cover and leave to rest for 10 minutes.

Divide the dough into 12 portions and roll each portion into a small ball.

Heat enough oil for deep-frying in a large, deep pan to 170°C (340°F) or until a cube of bread browns in 25 seconds when dropped into the oil. When the oil is hot enough, carefully lower the dough balls in batches into the hot oil and cook for 2–3 minutes until golden. Remove with a slotted spoon to drain on kitchen paper and leave to cool for 5 minutes.

Break up the dough balls and put them into a food processor. Blitz to coarse crumbs – don't make the mixture too fine.

To finish, heat the ghee in a frying pan over a medium heat, add the crumbs and cook for 4–5 minutes until the mixture is dry and crispy. Leave to cool for 5 minutes, then add the rest of the ingredients and mix well.

Serve at room temperature.

Our neighbours always used to bring coconut barfi for us on Diwali. These are very popular Indian sweets that can be made in numerous ways and are also available in a few pastel colours like pink and green. Here I have tried to recreate the flavours in this very simple recipe.

Nariyal barfi | Coconut barfi

SERVES 4

200g (7oz) fresh coconut

2 tablespoons ghee, plus extra for greasing

150ml (5fl oz) whole milk

70g (2½oz) soft brown sugar

seeds from 6–8 cardamom pods

a handful of pistachios, roughly chopped

Finely grate or blitz the fresh coconut in a food processor to a fine texture like desiccated coconut.

Heat the ghee in a saucepan, add the coconut and cook over a low–medium heat for 7 minutes until it starts to change colour. Add the milk and cook for 5 minutes until it has been absorbed, then add the sugar and cook for a further 10 minutes until all the liquid has been absorbed by the coconut and the mixture becomes dry and starts to leave the sides of the pan.

Crush the cardamom seeds in a pestle and mortar, add to the mixture in the pan and combine well.

Grease a small, deep baking tray, about 23 × 15cm (9 × 6 inches), with ghee, pour in the barfi mixture and spread it to 1cm (½ inch) thick. Sprinkle the pistachios on top and press them all in. Leave to cool completely before cutting into squares or rectangles.

You can store this in the refrigerator for 3–4 days, but it is best enjoyed on the day of making.

MENU PLANS

1

Makai cutlets | Corn cutlets (see page 27)
Palak paneer | Spinach paneer curry (see page 58)
Bharva shimla mirch | Stuffed peppers (see page 86)
Masaledar puri | Spiced-up puri (see page 123)
Veg tawa pulao (see page 144)
Chukandar raita | Beetroot raita (see page 181)
Balushahi (see page 189)

2

Till paneer | Sesame seed paneer fingers (see page 40)
Mixed dal (see page 101)
Bati | Baked dough balls (see page 116)
Hara adrak pulao | Green ginger pulao (see page 145)
Masala raita (see page 168)
Churma (see page 204)

3

Mirchi pakora | Chilli pakora (see page 36)

Baigan tamatar | Aubergine with tomatoes (see page 75)

Nariyal ka sambhar | Coconut sambhar (see page 104)

Palak paneer paratha | Spinach and paneer paratha
(see page 121)

Dahi chawal | Yogurt rice (see page 153)

Chiroti (see page 193)

4

Kela vada | Banana masala balls (see page 23)

Tari wale alu | Potato curry (see page 71)

Bedmi puri | Dal-stuffed puri (see page 134)

Vagharela bhaat | Onion rice (see page 158)

Masala raita (see page 168)

Puran poli laddoo (see page 197)

5

Aam ka salad | Mango slaw (see page 37)
Dahi wale pyaaz | Yogurt onion curry (see page 80)
Kala chana ghugni | Black chickpea curry (see page 95)
Masaledar puri | Spiced-up puri (see page 123)
Hara adrak pulao | Green ginger pulao (see page 145)
Gur chawal ki kheer | Jaggery rice kheer (see page 200)

6

Sindhi pakora (see page 22)
Chana dal (see page 90)
Pakwaan | Crispy pastries (see page 122)
Dhania chutney | Coriander and ginger chutney (see page 172)
Imli chutney | Tamarind chutney (see page 179)
Chukandar raita | Beetroot raita (see page 181)
Nariyal barfi | Coconut barfi (see page 205)

7

Aam ka salad | Mango slaw (see page 37)

Till ke alu | Sesame, peanut and potato sabzi (see page 56)

Chole | Chickpea curry (see page 100)

Bhatura (see page 129)

Gobhi raita | Roast cauliflower raita (see page 169)

Gur chawal ki kheer | Jaggery rice kheer (see page 200)

8

Tamatar ki chaat | Tomato chaat (see page 16)

Rainbow chard and pea sabzi (see page 62)

Chana madra | Chickpea yogurt curry (see page 111)

Sattu paratha | Gram flour-stuffed paratha (see page 128)

Sugar snap pea raita (see page 165)

Mirchi chutney | Chilli chutney (see page 173)

Sukdi | Jaggery treat (see page 186)

9

Palak muthiya | Crispy spinach (see page 43)
Mirchi ka salan | Chilli curry (see page 79)
Urad sabut dal | Black dal (see page 94)
Sabzi chole biryani | Vegetable and chickpea biryani (see page 148)
Masala raita (see page 168)
Nariyal barfi | Coconut barfi (see page 205)

10

Raj kachori (see page 30)
Veg tawa pulao (see page 144)
Masala raita (see page 168)
Chukandar raita | Beetroot raita (see page 181)
Sukdi | Jaggery treat (see page 186)

Glossary of UK/US terms

aubergine.................................eggplant

baking paper.......................parchment paper

baking/roasting tin..........baking/roasting pan

baking tray.............................baking sheet

barbecue................................grill

beetroots...............................beets

bicarbonate of soda.........baking soda

cake tin..................................cake pan

caster sugar.........................superfine sugar

chickpeas..............................garbanzo beans

chilli/chillies........................chili/chiles

chilli flakes...........................red pepper flakes

coriander (fresh)................cilantro

cornflour...............................cornstarch

courgette..............................zucchini

desiccated coconut...........unsweetened desiccated coconut (or substitute unsweetened shredded)

double cream.......................heavy cream

frying pan..............................skillet

gram flour.............................chickpea flour

green pepper........................green bell pepper

grill..broil/broiler

hob..stove

icing sugar............................confectioners' sugar

kitchen paper......................paper towels

plain flour.............................all-purpose flour

red pepper............................red bell pepper

shops......................................stores

sieve.......................................strainer

spring onions.......................scallions

stick blender........................immersion blender

sweetcorn.............................corn

tins..cans

tomato purée.......................tomato paste

Index

A

aam ka salad (mango slaw) 37
almonds
    churma 204
    jaggery rice kheer 200
    khaman ghari 190
alu bonda (masala potato balls)
    19
asparagus
    asparagus dal 107
    green ginger pulao 145
aubergines
    aubergine with tomatoes 75
    dal rice 155
    tomato chutney 166

B

baigan tamatar (aubergine with
    tomatoes) 75
bajra
    rotla 139
balushahi 189
banana masala balls 23
bati (baked dough balls) 116
beans, green
    vegetable and chickpea biryani
    148–9
bedmi puri (dal-stuffed puri) 134
beetroot
    beetroot raita 181
    veg tawa pulao 144
besan *see* gram flour
bhakri 133
bharva shimla mirch (stuffed
    peppers) 86
bhatura 129
black chickpea curry 95
black dal 94
bottle gourd chutney 180
breadcrumbs
    corn cutlets 27
    sesame seed paneer fingers
    40
bulgur wheat
    lapsi 203

C

cabbage
    lentil and onion vada 26
    mixed veg kofta curry 52
cardamom pods
    balushahi 189
    chickpea curry 100
    chiroti 193
    coconut barfi 205
    vegetable and chickpea biryani 148–9
carrots
    mixed veg kofta curry 52
    moong dal with carrots 106
    vegetable and chickpea biryani 148–9
    vegetable Kolhapuri 69
cashew nuts
    churma 204
    lapsi 203
    tomato chaat 16
    vegetable Kolhapuri 69
    yogurt rice 153
caster sugar
    balushahi 189
    chiroti 193
    khaman ghari 190
    lapsi 203
    Mysore pak 196
cauliflower
    masala rice 152
    roast cauliflower raita 169
    vegetable and chickpea biryani 148–9
chana dal 90
    chana dal and spinach 55
    mixed dal 101
    puran poli laddoo 197
    red pepper chutney 162
    sour white dhokla 34
chana madra (chickpea yogurt curry) 111
chapatti flour
    baked dough balls 116
    bhakri 133
    churma 204
    crispy spinach 43
    dal-stuffed puri 134
    fenugreek flatbreads 135

    gram flour-stuffed paratha 128
    jaggery treat 186
    onion paratha 117
    rotla 139
    seeded roti 114
    spiced-up crispy pastry 20
    spiced-up puri 123
    spinach and paneer paratha 121
chickpeas
    black chickpea curry 95
    chickpea curry 100
    chickpea yogurt curry 111
    vegetable and chickpea biryani 148–9
chillies
    banana masala balls 23
    black chickpea curry 95
    bottle gourd chutney 180
    chickpea yogurt curry 111
    chilli chutney 173
    chilli curry 79
    chilli pakora 36
    coriander and ginger chutney 172
    fenugreek balls 48
    fenugreek flatbreads 135
    instant rice dosa 126
    mixed dal 101
    onion and garlic chutney 176
    onion paratha 117
    potato curry 71
    rotla 139
    sesame, peanut and potato sabzi 56
    simply spiced whole moong dal 9
    spinach and paneer paratha 121
    sugar snap pea raita 165
    tomato chutney 166
    veg tawa pulao 144
    vegetable Kolhapuri 69
    yogurt rice 153
chiroti 193
chole (chickpea curry) 100
chukandar raita (beetroot raita) 181
churma 204
coconut
    chilli curry 79
    coconut barfi 205

coconut sambhar 104
khaman ghari 190
lapsi 203
masala rice 142
puran poli laddoo 197
red pepper chutney 162
coriander and ginger chutney 172
corn cutlets 27
courgettes
courgette and sweet potato sabzi 70
poppadam and courgette yogurt curry 74
crispy pastries 122
crispy spinach 43

D
dahi bhindi (yogurt and okra sabzi) 83
dahi chawal (yogurt rice) 153
dahi wale pyaaz (yogurt onion curry) 80
dal rice 155
dal-stuffed puri 134
dates
tamarind chutney 179
dhania chutney (coriander and ginger
chutney) 172
drumsticks *see* moringa

F
fenugreek and gram flour curry 99
fenugreek balls 48
fenugreek flatbreads 135
flour *see* chapatti flour; gram flour;
plain flour; rice flour

G
garlic
chilli chutney 173
onion and garlic chutney 176
ghee
baked dough balls 116
balushahi 189
churma 204
jaggery treat 186
khaman ghari 190
lapsi 203
Mysore pak 196

rotla 139
sugar snap pea raita 165
ghegho (fenugreek and gram flour curry)
99
ginger
coriander and ginger chutney 172
crispy spinach 43
green ginger pulao 145
masala raita 168
gobhi raita (roast cauliflower raita) 169
gram flour
banana masala balls 23
chilli pakora 36
fenugreek and gram flour curry 99
fenugreek balls 48
gram flour-stuffed paratha 128
masala potato balls 19
Mysore pak 196
pepper pakora 45
Sindhi pakora 22
tomato sabzi 63
granulated sugar
ras malai 192
green ginger pulao 145
gur chawal ki kheer (jaggery rice kheer)
200

H
hara adrak pulao (green ginger pulao) 145

I
imli chutney (tamarind chutney) 179
Indoori poha 44
instant rice dosa 126

J
jaggery
jaggery rice kheer 200
jaggery treat 186
puran poli laddoo 197
tamarind chutney 179

K
kadambam (dal rice) 155
kala chana ghugni (black chickpea curry) 95

kara chutney (onion and garlic chutney)
176
kela vada (banana masala balls) 23
keri bateki (mango potatoes) 66
khaman ghari 190
khatta dhokla (sour white dhokla) 34
koki (onion paratha) 117

L
lacchko moong (simply spiced whole
moong dal) 93
lal shimla mirch chutney (red pepper
chutney) 162
lapsi 203
lauki chutney (bottle gourd chutney) 180
lentils
black dal 94
dal-stuffed puri 134
lentil and onion vada 26
mixed dal 101
puran poli laddoo 197
red pepper chutney 162
sugar snap pea raita 165

M
makai cutlets (corn cutlets) 27
mango potatoes 66
mango slaw 37
masala potato balls 19
masala raita 168
masala rice 142
masaledar puri (spiced-up puri) 123
methi gota (fenugreek balls) 48
milk
coconut barfi 205
jaggery rice kheer 200
ras malai 192
vegetable and chickpea biryani 148–9
mirchi chutney (chilli chutney) 173
mirchi ki salan (chilli curry) 79
mirchi pakora (chilli pakora) 36
mixed dal 101
mixed veg kofta curry 52
moong dal
chana dal 90

dal rice 155
mixed dal 101
moong dal with carrots 106
raj kachori 30-1
simply spiced whole moong dal 93
spinach rice 154
moringa
coconut sambhar 104
dal rice 155
mung beans *see* moong dal
Mysore pak 196

N

namak para (spiced-up crispy pastry) 20
nariyal barfi (coconut barfi) 205
nariyal ka sambhar (coconut sambhar)
104
nuts
bottle gourd chutney 180
chilli curry 79
churma 204
coconut barfi 205
jaggery rice kheer 200
jaggery treat 186
khaman ghari 190
lapsi 203
ras malai 192
sesame, peanut and potato sabzi 56
tomato chaat 16
vegetable Kolhapuri 69
yogurt rice 153

O

okra
yogurt and okra sabzi 83
onions
aubergine with tomatoes 75
black dal 94
coconut sambhar 104
gram flour-stuffed paratha 12
green ginger pulao 145
instant rice dosa 126
lentil and onion vada 26
mango slaw 37
masala raita 168
mixed veg kofta curry 52
onion and garlic chutney 176
onion paratha 117
onion rice 158

rainbow chard and pea sabzi 62
rotla 139
Sindhi pakora 22
spinach paneer curry 58
veg tawa pulao 144
vegetable and chickpea biryani 148-9
vegetable Kolhapuri 69
yogurt and okra sabzi 83
yogurt onion curry 80

P

pakora
chilli pakora 36
pepper pakora 45
Sindhi pakora 22
pakwaan (crispy pastries) 122
palak ki khichdi (spinach rice) 154
palak muthiya (crispy spinach) 43
palak paneer (spinach paneer curry)
58
palak paneer paratha (spinach and
paneer paratha) 121
paneer
scrambled paneer and peas 82
sesame seed paneer fingers 40
spinach and paneer paratha 121
spinach paneer curry 58
vegetable Kolhapuri 69
paneer matar bhurji (scrambled paneer
and peas) 82
papad kadhi (poppadam and courgette
yogurt curry) 74
pastries
chiroti 193
crispy pastries 122
spiced-up crispy pastry 20
peanuts
bottle gourd chutney 180
chilli curry 79
sesame, peanut and potato sabzi 56
pearl millet flour *see* bajra
peas
green ginger pulao 145
masala rice 142
rainbow chard and pea sabzi 62
sugar snap pea raita 165
vegetable Kolhapuri 69
peas, pigeon split *see* toor dal
peas, yellow split *see* chana dal

peppers
instant rice dosa 126
pepper pakora 45
red pepper chutney 162
stuffed peppers 86
veg tawa pulao 144
vegetable Kolhapuri 69
pistachios
coconut barfi 205
jaggery rice kheer 200
jaggery treat 186
ras malai 192
plain flour
balushahi 189
chiroti 193
crispy pastries 122
khaman ghari 190
poppadam and courgette yogurt curry
74
potatoes
chilli pakora 36
dal rice 155
mango potatoes 66
masala potato balls 19
masala rice 142
mixed veg kofta curry 52
potato curry 71
sesame, peanut and potato sabzi 56
stuffed peppers 86
tomato chaat 16
veg tawa pulao 144
vegetable and chickpea biryani 148-9
puran poli laddoo 197

R

rainbow chard and pea sabzi 62
raisins
jaggery rice kheer 200
khaman ghari 190
lapsi 203
raj kachori 30-1
ras malai 192
red pepper chutney 162
rice
dal rice 155
green ginger pulao 145
Indoori poha 44
jaggery rice kheer 200
masala rice 142

onion rice 158
    puran poli laddoo 197
    sour white dhokla 34
    spinach rice 154
    veg tawa pulao 144
    vegetable and chickpea biryani 148–9
    yogurt rice 153
rice flour
    instant rice dosa 126
    spiced-up puri 123
rotla 139

S

sabzi chole biryani (vegetable and chickpea biryani) 148–9
sai bhaji (chana dal and spinach) 55
sattu paratha (gram flour-stuffed paratha) 128
scrambled paneer and peas 82
seeded roti 114
semolina
    bhatura 129
    chiroti 193
    crispy pastries 122
    dal-stuffed puri 134
    raj kachori 30–1
sesame seeds
    sesame seed paneer fingers 40
    sesame, peanut and potato sabzi 56
sev tameta nu shaak (tomato sabzi) 63
shallots
    coconut sambhar 104
    yogurt onion curry 80
Sindhi pakora 22
sour white dhokla 34
spices
    simply spiced whole moong dal 93
    spiced-up crispy pastry 20
    spiced-up puri 123
    see tadka (tempering spices)
spinach
    chana dal and spinach 55
    crispy spinach 43
    spinach and paneer paratha 121
    spinach paneer curry 58
    spinach rice 154
spring onions
    green ginger pulao 145
    rotla 139

stuffed peppers 86
sugar snap pea raita 165
sugar
    churma 204
    coconut barfi 205
    see caster sugar; granulated sugar; jaggery
sukdi (jaggery treat) 186
sweet potatoes
    courgette and sweet potato sabzi 70
sweetcorn
    corn cutlets 27

T

tadka (tempering spices)
    banana masala balls 23
    beetroot raita 181
    bottle gourd chutney 180
    chana dal 90
    coconut sambhar 104
    crispy spinach 43
    dal rice 155
    mango potatoes 66
    masala raita 168
    mixed dal 101
    moong dal with carrots 106
    onion and garlic chutney 176
    red pepper chutney 162
    spinach paneer curry 58
    spinach rice 154
    yogurt rice 153
tamarind
    chickpea curry 100
    chilli curry 79
    coconut sambhar 104
    dal rice 155
    tamarind chutney 179
tamatar chutney (tomato chutney) 166
tamatar ki chaat (tomato chaat) 16
tari wale alu (potato curry) 71
thepla (fenugreek flatbreads) 135
till ke alu (sesame, peanut and potato sabzi) 56
till paneer (sesame seed paneer fingers) 40
tomatoes
    aubergine with tomatoes 75
    bottle gourd chutney 180
    chana dal and spinach 55

chilli chutney 173
    masala raita 168
    mixed veg kofta curry 52
    onion and garlic chutney 176
    scrambled paneer and peas 82
    tomato chaat 16
    tomato chutney 166
    tomato sabzi 63
    veg tawa pulao 144
    vegetable and chickpea biryani 148–9
    vegetable Kolhapuri 69
    yogurt onion curry 80
toor dal
    asparagus dal 107
    coconut sambhar 104
    dal rice 155
    mixed dal 101
    sour white dhokla 34

U

urad dal pyaaz vada (lentil and onion vada) 26
urad sabut dal (black dal) 94

V

vagharela bhaat (onion rice) 158
veg tawa pulao 144
vegetable and chickpea biryani 148–9
vegetable Kolhapuri 69

Y

yogurt
    balushahi 189
    beetroot raita 181
    bhatura 129
    chickpea yogurt curry 111
    instant rice dosa 126
    masala raita 168
    poppadam and courgette yogurt curry 74
    raj kachori 30–1
    roast cauliflower raita 169
    sour white dhokla 34
    sugar snap pea raita 165
    vegetable and chickpea biryani 148–9
    yogurt and okra sabzi 83
    yogurt onion curry 80
    yogurt rice 153

Acknowledgements

This book would have not been possible without the love and warmth of so many people in India, who generously gave me their time, opened their homes and hearts to welcome a stranger and let me watch them create magic in their space. And all of that would have not been possible without Sheetal Bhatt. Thank you also to the amazing ladies in Ahmedabad who shared their family recipes with me: Avani, Meena Aunty, Bhumika, Kety Aunty, Renuka, Shimul and Ranjan Aunty.

I am also grateful to my college friend Lakshmi and her mum Subbalakshmi for sharing their cooking knowledge with me. Massive thanks to my cousin Nimisha, who not only looked after me in Mumbai but also shared her mother-in-law's recipe secrets with me. And to my local friend Radhika for always feeding me her delicious food and sharing her recipes with me.

Big thanks to my Editorial Director, Natalie Bradley, for your constant support and for always giving your time to hear all my ideas and suggestions, for which I am grateful.

Thanks to the amazing team behind the book: Art Director Juliette Norsworthy, who spends a whole lot of time creating the perfect colour schemes and designs to go with my recipes; Senior Editor Leanne Bryan, who has such a sharp eye and gets everything spot on every single time; and the amazing Publicity team, Ailie and Hazel, who put in so much time and effort to spread the word for the book. Thanks also to Emily Preece-Morrison, who took control of the editing and made it all make sense. Big thanks to the whole team at Octopus for all your hard work.

Thank you to the very talented Nassima Rothacker, who has photographed every single book of mine. She pours so much love and care into each photograph, bringing the food to life in the way only she can. Thanks to Rosie Reynolds, the Food Stylist for the book, who understands my recipes with ease and cooks them with so much love and expertise. The book shoot days with this team are ones I look forward to while writing the book.

Thanks to all my friends for always being my cheerleaders, whatever I get up to.

And, most importantly, thank you to my family – to my husband Gaurav and kids Sia and Yuv, who really are the people living the book with me, eating all the food for months. They are so amazing when I am in the bubble of book writing that I could not do it without their immense love and support.

About the author

Chetna Makan was born in Jabalpur in Central India. She has a degree in fashion and worked in Mumbai as a fashion designer before moving to the UK in 2004. Chetna was part of *The Great British Bake Off* in 2014 and since then has written eight cookbooks. They range from baking, Indian street food and healthy Indian food to vegetarian and quick Indian. She also has a very popular YouTube channel 'Food with Chetna' where she shares her creative flair for all things cooking and baking. She has previously collaborated with Jamie Oliver and Waitrose.

www.chetnamakan.co.uk
instagram.com/chetnamakan
twitter.com/chetnamakan
youtube.com/FoodwithChetna
facebook.com/chetna.makan

Other titles by Chetna Makan

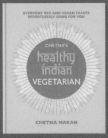

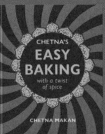
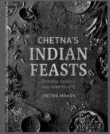